# Disco

*Disco*

*by* Albert Goldman

**HAWTHORN BOOKS, INC.** *Publishers/*New York  *A Howard & Wyndham Company*

DISCO

Copyright © 1978 by Shpritzgun Productions. Copyright under International and Pan-American Copyright Conventions. All rights reserved, including the right to reproduce this book or portions thereof in any form, except for the inclusion of brief quotations in a review. All inquiries should be addressed to Hawthorn Books, Inc., 260 Madison Avenue, New York, New York 10016. This book was manufactured in the United States of America and published simultaneously in Canada by Prentice-Hall of Canada, Limited, 1870 Birchmount Road, Scarborough, Ontario.

Library of Congress Catalog Card Number: 78-70002
ISBN: 0-8015-2128-9
1  2  3  4  5  6  7  8  9  10

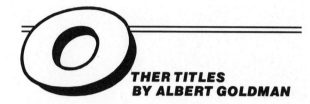

OTHER TITLES
BY ALBERT GOLDMAN

*Carnival in Rio*

*The Mine and the Mint: Sources for the Writings of
Thomas DeQuincey*

*Wagner on Music and Drama* (co-editor with
Everett Sprinchorn)

*Freakshow: The Rocksoulbluesjazzsickjewblack-
humorsexpoppsych Gig and Other Scenes from the
Counter-Culture*

*Ladies and Gentlemen—LENNY BRUCE!!!*

**FOR RENE LACHICOTTE**

# Acknowledgments

Grateful acknowledgment is made to the following people and organizations that provided valuable information on disco: Francis Grasso; Vince Aletti; Ed and Michael Gifford and Wendy Littlefield of Gifford and Wallace; Teddy Graham of Philadelphia International; Alex Kabazz, Brad Le Beau, Alfredo Zucaro, and Nicole Semhon of *Discothekin'*; Larry Silverman; Olivier Coquelin; Régine and Flora of Régine's; Terry Noel; Dicken Acramen; Ronnie Sanders; Beth Wernick of Levinson Associates; Tom Moulton; Jim Burgess; Jerry Brandt; Doug Riddick of Private Stock; David Rodriguez of Butterfly Records; Philip LoCascio; Bob Siegel; Ray Caviano and Janet Oseroff of T.K. Records; Steve Keator, Mark Simon, Bea Frankel, and Roberta Skop of Casablanca Records; Steven Baker of Epic Records; Howard Levitt of *Record World*; Luigi and Ronnie DeMarco of Luigi's Dance Studio; Killer Joe Piro; Drew Nugent; Alec Costandinos; Bob Edson and Kevin McCormick of the Robert Stigwood Organization; Jerry Wexler, Israel Sanchez, and Jo Ann Toker of Atlantic Records; Raquel Cortez of ABC Records; Nikki Siano; Lorraine Chamberlain; Andy Warhol and Bob Colacello of *Interview*; Sybil Burton; Jim McMullan; Fred Gitner of the French Institute; Jo Ann Horowitz of Xenon; Steve Rubell and Michael Overington of Studio 54; Michael Giammetta, Frank Schmitt, Stefan Verk, and Steve Alterwein of *Michael's Thing*; Jules Fisher and Paul Marantz; Philip Miles; Bob Tisch; Richard Gersh and Bonnie Zucker of Richard Gersh Associates; Harry Spiro of Mid-Song Records; Meco Monardo; Tom Sullivan; Catherine Guinness; Janet Weber of Rocket Records; The Power Station; David Carey; Jean-Paul Goude; New York Hustle, Inc.; Head Limos of Queens; Charles Rusinak of 2001 Odyssey; Mel Adelglass; Jane Krupp; Brian Lantelme; Howard A. Levine and Bill Kenly of Paramount Pictures; Oskana Makarushka of *Rolling Stone*; Michael Gomes of *Mixmaster*; Michel de Chabert-Ostland; Walter Gibbons of Salsoul Records; Charles Comer of Island Records; Sheila Berger Wolfe of *Harper's* magazine; Barry Secunda; Antonio; Laurence Madrille; Richard Merkin; Denis Wright; Merle Peek.

Especially, thanks are due to Ben Sims, Barry Berkman, and to the indefatigable efforts of Sonia Moskowitz and my editorial assistant, Charlotte Lyons.

**Design Director: Kenneth Kneitel**
**Designers: Diana La Guardia, Fred Weiss**
**Photo Researcher: Annie Toglia**
**Production Assistant: Amy Malina**

WHEN [the Australian aborigines] come together, a sort of electricity is formed by their collecting which quickly transports them to an extraordinary degree of exaltation. Every sentiment expressed finds a place without resistance in all the minds... each re-echoes the others, and is re-echoed ...The initial impulse thus proceeds, growing as it goes, as an avalanche grows in its advance. And as such active passions so free from all control could not fail to burst out...one sees nothing but violent gestures, cries, veritable howls, and deafening noises of every sort. ...These gestures and cries naturally tend to become rhythmic and regular; hence come songs and dances. The human voice is not sufficient for the task. It is reinforced by means of artificial processes: boomerangs are beaten against each other; bull-roarers are whirled.

This effervescence often reaches such a point that it causes unheard-of actions. The passions released are of such impetuosity that they can be restrained by nothing....The sexes unite contrarily to the rules governing sexual relations. Men exchange wives with each other. Sometimes even incestuous unions, which in normal times are thought abominable and are severely punished, are now contracted openly and with impunity. If we add to all this that the ceremonies generally take place at night in a darkness pierced here and there by the light of fires, we can easily imagine...such experiences...leave [the participants with] the conviction that there really exist two heterogeneous and mutually incomparable worlds.

One is that where his daily life drags wearily along; the other [is where he enters] into relations with extraordinary powers that excite him to the point of frenzy. The first is the profane world, the second, that of sacred things....So it is in the midst of these effervescent social environments and out of this effervescence itself that the religious idea seems to be born.

Émile Durkheim
*The Elementary Forms of the Religious Life*

T'S New Year's Eve at Studio 54—the hottest ticket in town. All night, even as you relished your little supper of beluga caviar and Dom Perignon, or as you rolled across the wire-strung, cathedral-arched Bridge to visit friends in the nineteenth-century dream of Brooklyn Heights, or as you laughed and joked, tooted and toked with the glowing girls in the back seat of your big black limo, you've been pointing to that moment when you'd be piped aboard the flagship of New York's Great White Fleet of spaceship discotheques. When you'd shoulder through the mob of gape-mouthed groundlings and pass inside the palace of pleasure, just like the old movie stars used to do at their searchlight-crossed Hollywood premieres. Days ago you got the word that nothing would be happening at the club till 3:00 A.M.; so you've laid back this Eve, postponing your peak of pleasure in anticipation of the big climax. Now it's coming.

Up the nearly deserted Eighth Avenue you roll on heavy rubber, keen yet mellow, feeling like those supremely confident boxers who doze on the rubbing table before they step into the ring. As you slow down for the final turn at 54th Street, you feel a little trickle of excitement. You pat the breast pocket of your evening jacket, checking to see that you've got that little round film can of blow. Then—*god-damn-it-to-hell!*—you stick fast in a traffic jam!

Peering out the window, you see a strange sight. Instead of the cars and cabs, garbage trucks and delivery vans, heating-oil tankers and tattooed dump trucks that normally clog New York's apoplectic arteries, this pileup consists entirely of *limousines*. Big, long, black, brown, or beige undertakers' cars. Why, it looks like the final rites of Toledo Teddy out in Bensonhurst or Big Nig up in Harlem. Right there, angling to cut across your right fender, is a fantastic-looking, cinnamon-colored, stretched-out, custom-built Lincoln Continental, with a spray of TV and FM antennas raked back from its trunk like the communications gear on a satellite. "Christ!" you think. "It's just like the days of the Great White

1

Way and the Manhattan Merry-Go-Round. I might as well be Jay Gatsby—or that Hebe who fixed the World Series!"

Shouting last-minute instructions to the driver, you duck out and slice through the crowd pressing against the red plush movie lobby ropes. All of New York's practiced gate-crashers are giving it their best try tonight. From every side they flash their smiles, drop their names, run their scams on the doorman. "Mark! Remember me from the David Bowie party?"..."I beg your pardon, I'm from the *New York Times*"..."Please, Mistah! Dontcha' unnerstan'? I'm Herbie's *girlfren'*—he's *expectin'* me!"

Studio 54 is a private club. That gives them a license to discriminate. Discrimination is the name of their game. Not the subtle WASPy discrimination of the old Stork Club or El Morocco, but the blatant *you*-can-come-in-but-*you*-gotta-stay-out style of an eight-year-old's treehouse. All night long, Mark, the blond, elegant, willowy maitre d'street, has been standing bareheaded out in the cold, flanked by his flunkies and backed by his man-mountain muscle, picking and choosing, barring and losing. His job is the most important one in the whole joint. It even has a special name. It's called "painting the picture."

Painting the picture is the secret of a successful

disco operation. You don't get to be the No. 1 hot spot in New York just by installing eighty thousand dollars worth of lighting equipment or seventy thousand dollars worth of burgundy-red British broadloom or even by getting some post-grad sound engineer with steel-rimmed spectacles to design you a special custom-built hi-fi system with enough decibels to smash your inner ear to oyster jelly but so soft and stimulating in actual effect that it makes you feel like you've stepped into a supersonic vapor bath. No, what makes a joint like Studio 54 the vortex of New York's whirling night life is not so much the accommodations as the crowd and not so much the crowd that turns up as the way this ever-changing melee of fashionably costumed, strikingly good-looking, celebrity-studded young men and women is selected, composed, and matched up every night. When these thousands of randomly arriving strangers bump into each other on the vast dance floor or on the black-striped, silver gas-tank cushions of the downstairs lounge or up in the dusky-crimson bordello parlor of the smoking lounge, it is preordained that they will virtually fall into each other's arms, with the head-on excitement of love at first sight.

The basic scenario is simple. First, they dance, dance, dance, till their legs go into cramps. Then they snort, snort, snort, till their teeth are numb and their heads about to fly off. Then, some of them get so hot to slot that they run up into the great, dark, steep balcony that lowers over the dance floor like a massive thunderhead. And there, with Halston gowns wrenching and tearing and St. Laurent velvet tuxedos popping their buttons, the flower of New York's party people *get it on,* while around them sprawl the luded-out voyeurs who dig these scenes like strokers in a 42nd Street grindhouse.

Tonight, the picture has to be painted pink because Studio 54, flush with the millions it earned during its fabulously successful first year of operation, is offering its favorite customers a very special treat: nothing less than the Queen of Disco, Grace Jones, performing all her recent hits in a smashing floor show, complete with sets, costumes, dance routines—the whole Josephine Baker trip. Grace is the reigning queen not only of disco but of the New York gays, who are disco's hard-core devotees. These are the boys who kept the beat going during the dull, doldrummed early

seventies, when the straight world had stopped dancing and sat around asking itself: "Whatever happened to the sixties?" Though Studio 54 normally caters to a predominantly straight white crowd (with just a few token blacks and token grays), tonight the joint will be flooded with boychicks with cropped hair, beards, punk outfits, safety pins, razor blades, and coke jitters.

As you quick-step through the towering foyer of what was once the Fortune Gallo Opera House

(later, a CBS studio for *What's My Line?*), you notice that the ghostly silver-sprayed TV boom camera has been removed along with the sixteen-foot fig trees and their place taken by a bevy of squat little machines that blow an endless profusion of prismatically colored bubbles. There's no time now to dig the party decorations because you're racing toward the mighty magnet that draws and drives the fastest human particles in New York: the great spaceship dance hall where Mick and Bianca, Andy and Halston, Liza and Margaret, Nureyev and Barishnykov, Truman and Elton get down like cats and kitties at a Bed-Stuy rent party.

## FLOOR SHOW

**A**S you swing around the corner and confront the floor, you're struck head on by a very heavy disco mix called *Devil's Gun*. With a concussive tympanic roll, the number kicks off: "*Bruuuumph!* FEE FIIIIE! FOE FUHMB! YO LOOKIN' DOWN DA BARREL O' DA DE-BIL'S GUN! *Bruuuumph!* NO-WHAAAARE TO RUN! YA GOT-TA MAKE A STAN' AGINST DE DE-BIL'S GUN!" Roaring like King Kong in rut, the colossal boogie voice booms into the darkness. The floor, virtually blacked out, is lit intermittently by flashes of lightning and thrummed with claps of thunder. You feel like you've crashed in the Congo—between the elements and the animals, you don't stand a chance.

Suddenly, with channel-selector abruptness, the image flips from the *Heart of Darkness* to Times Square. Winking-blinking, racing-chasing marquee lights bedazzle your eyes. As these Broadway fireworks ignite the night, you take

another fix on the scene. This time your mind flashes: "Cape Canaveral at ground zero!"

Directly before you stands a squadron of towering, pencil-shaped rockets fashioned of chrome wire and studded with pulsing, patterned red and yellow lights. Suddenly, the fuckers start to slide up into the dark overhead, kissing off the earth with a parting volley from their flashing rotary taillights. As you gaze through the murk at the dancers thrashing around like a befuddled ground crew, all hell breaks loose. *Zap! Zap! Zap! Zap!* A score of blinding strobes is raking the floor. Fluid motion is freeze-dried into blue-

white snapshots. *Zap! Zap! Zap! Zap!* Your brain is starting to reel. You feel you're flying while standing still. Then the back wall of the hangar lights up—and you crack up!

You're gaping at a fascinatingly funny apparition looming luridly on the disco's back wall. It's Old Man Moon! That emaciated crescent-profiled old fool! How his toothless, senescent jaw juts up until it practically touches the tip of his pendant coxcomb! Drooping from the middle of his concave punim hangs his tired old hose nose, detumescent, like a spent shlong. Wait! Help is coming! A surrealistically distended coke spoon is thrust under the Moon's limp shnozz. White, bright bubbles like cocaine race up his elephantine proboscis. The bubbles fly as high as the Moon's evil red eye. The dancers scream! The beat booms louder. The floor fibrillates. Then the whole discotheque comes to climax.

Down from the dark heavens comes a thick, soft fall of snow. Thousands of feathery white flakes fluttering down upon the milling figures below. Pennies from heaven. Bennies from heaven. Now nose candy from the Andes. It's a stunning disco Xmas card. A snow-blind Currier & Ives.

## AMAZING GRACE

**T**HAT'S it, boys and girls! Everybody off the floor now. The automated show is over and the live show is about to begin. As the springy-legged ushers, stripped down to white satin boxer shorts, clear the decks, everyone's gaze focuses upon a huge cobra head, whose lurid red eyes gaze menacingly from the back of the dancing area. As the cathedral sound system starts to belt out Grace Jones's theme song, *I Need A Man,* through the monster's gaping mouth come slithering one by one Grace Jones's famous chorus line of dancing boys. Tonight they're in s/m drag: black jockstraps and matching shoulder holsters. The twelve boys form in a line and drop to one knee, holding out their automatics with both hands à la James Bond. If they could just squeeze the triggers and kill a few of the foremost spectators the effect would be perfect. Instead, they rise and turn to display their cinched-up asses, which they rotate slowly, giving their buns that mean, hard little grind that gets the crowd wild. The lads in front of you are now doing the gay-boy bunny hop as they prance frantically in place, packed into a dense cordon around the floor.

As the music builds to a peak of excitement, a grand puff of smoke belches from the mouth of the cobra. Materializing abruptly amidst the fumes is SHE—the Disco Goddess. Looking like an African sculpture swathed in a gold lamé space

gown, Amazing Grace thrusts her cruel cat face, an evilly glaring mask, at the audience. As the chorus boys strut their stuff, the one-time fashion model goes into her act, silver mike in hand, belting out her tunes in a husky, loud, genuinely unmusical voice. First she strikes one pose, then another even more provocative. As she goes from tune to tune, strut to butt, her partners swagger round her like harem guards or fawn submissively beneath her gold boots like harem slaves. Gradually, her clothes come off. Finally, she's down to a gold diaper. Now she displays arrogantly before the hungry eyes of her admirers her classic African body. The long, skinny shanks, the abruptly flaring thighs, the spidery arms, and the tight fisticuff breasts. When the gold helmet comes off her predatory panther face, you see her skull knotted painfully into cornrows.

Now her rock-hard, black body is being fondled like a tribal fetish. Revealed and concealed, caressed and chastised, worshipped and defiled. She is held out as the ultimate symbol of the female principle, the feline essence, the cat goddess before whom every gay must prostrate himself in envy and adoration. With a last burst of smoke and sound and light, the apotheosis concludes. The goddess vanishes. The light-studded industrial totem poles descend upon the dance floor. The needle drops into a fresh groove, and — presto!—the discotheque is restored to its normal state as an immense can of frantically wriggling worms.

## DISCOMANIA

NOT every night in a New York disco is New Year's Eve, but every night there is plenty of action as disco becomes America's foremost form of live entertainment and participatory culture. In just one short year, disco exploded from an underground scene down on the New York waterfront or out in the boros and barrios into a vast international entertainment industry. Today, disco is right up there with spectator sports, tennis, and skiing as one of the most ideally contemporary forms of recreation. Specially composed and recorded disco music plays night and day on disco-oriented radio stations in every city of the country. Lavishly equipped disco entertainment centers are springing up all over the world like supermarkets. Disco stars like Barry White, Donna Summer, and Grace Jones are competing evermore successfully with the fading stars of rock. The first of the disco movies, *Saturday Night Fever,* set a new standard for financial success, and its soundtrack album has doubled the sales record of the Beatles' *Sergeant Pepper.* Disco is a four-billion-dollar-a-year industry, with its own franchises, publications, top-forty charts, three-day sales conventions, catalogues of special equipment, and keenly competitive marketing agents—who are aiming to make every finished basement and rumpus room in America into a mini-disco. The new beat for the feet is sending up all the familiar signals that betoken a new wave of mass culture.

The reasons for this unexpected triumph are not hard to discover once you start looking for them. The foremost reason is simply the fact that disco stands to the seventies in much the same relation as rock stood to the sixties: as a profoundly emblematic expression of a new world. The current decade, so slow to declare itself, has finally crystallized as a fascinating amalgam of hip and square, conservative and radical, primitive and futuristic. On the one hand, it's now hip to be square—to be self-disciplined, self-denying, hardworking, hard-driving, keen on getting ahead in either the race against your fellow

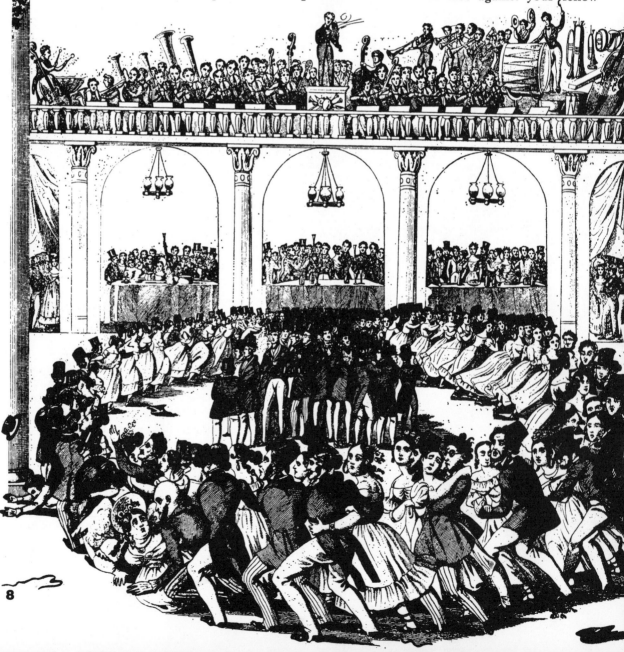

*The Grand Galop by Johann Strauss*
Viennese Theatrical Journal, *1839*

cerned is the mating game. The songs, which are written to formulas like the old Tin Pan Alley products, are directed ostensibly at a lover, typically someone the singer has just spotted on the dance floor. But the real thrust of disco culture is not toward love of another person but toward love of self — the principal object of desire in this age of closed-circuit, masturbatory vibrator sex. Outside the entrance to every discotheque should be erected a statue to the presiding deity: Narcissus.

## BALL THE WALL

LOOKING out on the floor of the modern dance hall, you don't see any of the interpersonal intimacy so glowingly described in the fashion magazines or on the screen during *Saturday Night Fever* (which like all Hollywood efforts to deal with current fads is hopelessly out of date). The idea that disco has been built on a revival of "touch dancing" (what a hideously clammy word!) or that it is focused on a step called the Latin Hustle is either wishful thinking by Arthur Murray instructors or just bad women's-page journalism. The truth is that today's hip disco dancer is into the kind of one-man show that John Travolta puts on in the most exciting sequence of *Saturday Night Fever*: a scene that speaks the truth despite itself. It unwittingly demonstrates how totally fulfilling it is to dance alone and how frustrating and infuriating it is to have to work out something as intimate as the way you dance with some cranky bitch.

Everybody sees himself as a star today. This is both a cliché and a profound truth. Thousands of young men and women have the looks, the clothes, the hairstyling, the drugs, the personal magnetism, the self-confidence, and the history of conquest that proclaim a star. The one thing they lack—talent—is precisely what is most lacking in those other, nearly identical, young people, whom the world has acclaimed as stars. Never in the history of show biz has the gap between amateur and professional been so small. And never in the history of the world has there been such a rage for exhibitionism. The question is, therefore, what are we going to do with all these

beautiful show-offs? Disco provides the best answer to date. Every night the stage is set, the lights are lit, and the audience is assembled; the floor will clear magically for anyone who really is intent on getting out there and doing his solo version of *Soul Train*. That's what makes the modern discotheque so different from the traditional ballroom: The people out on the floor are really serious about their dancing and are determined to do their thing — whether it be Fred Astaire, James Brown, or a whirling dervish —just as far as their well-conditioned bodies will carry them.

Getting yourself up to do your thing, however, is not such a simple matter — as any professional will confirm. Self-expression is less a matter of mood, energy, practice, and pep pills than it is of feeling that the people around you are *with* you. The hippies solved this problem by making the world into a giant sandbox where they could shit in their pants or piss down their legs and there would be no mamma to reprove them. The highly burnished people that are the disco droids have adopted a more traditional expedient. They have founded countless psychedelic country clubs smack in the heart of the big city where they can revel in the supportiveness of their own crowd. After the anarchic hugger-mugger of the sixties, Americans are back into segregation (a trend that was launched, incidentally, by blacks, not whites). Since there are so many races, classes, and cliques demanding to be segregated in any big American city, the number and variety of these exclusive dancing clubs has to be enormous. Recently, *Discothekin'* magazine estimated that in New York City alone there are 1,500 discotheques: discos for straights and gays, for blacks and Puerto Ricans, for poor slum teen-agers and rich middle-aged tourists.

## THE VARIETIES OF DISCO EXPERIENCE

AT Régine's, on Park Avenue, the prosperous Europeans that come pouring into New York looking for travel bargains and investment opportunities can well afford the nine

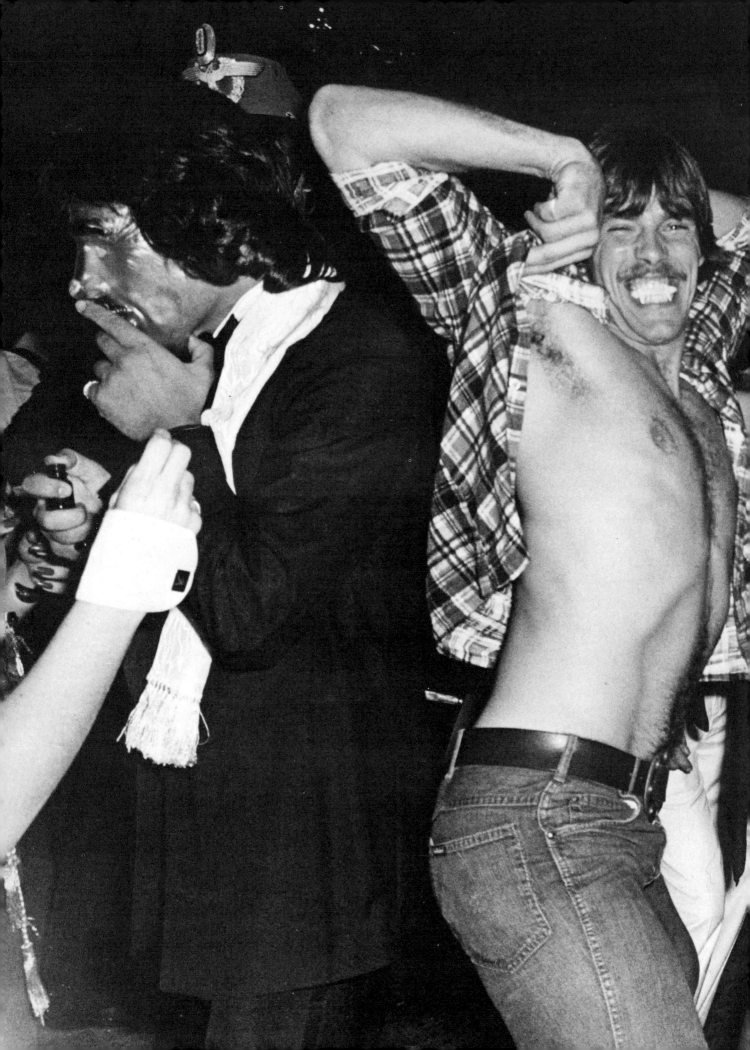

# 22 DISCOS

*From the caves of Paris to the factory lofts of New York, disco has always flourished best in an underground setting known only to its intimates. Arriving past midnight in some godforsaken neighborhood with nothing to guide him but a slip of paper bearing a scribbled address, the hard-core disco droid seeks his pleasure like the patron of an old-time speakeasy or opium den. The following pages illustrate some of the most celebrated but most secluded hot spots in the disco Casbah.*

down on the docks (the gays' happy hunting ground). As you climb its steeply angled ramp to the second floor, which is illuminated only by rows of sinister little red eyes, you feel like a character in a Kafka novel. From overhead comes the heavy pounding of the disco beat like a fearful migraine. When you reach the "bar," a huge bare parking area, you are astonished to see immense pornographic murals of Greek and Trojan warriors locked in sado-masochistic combat running from floor to ceiling. On the floor of the main dancing room are the most frenzied dancers on the disco scene: The black and Puerto Rican gays, stripped down to singlets and denim shorts, swing their bodies with wild abandon, while from their hip pockets flow foot-long sweat rags that fly like horses' tails.

Pushing out beyond the confines of Manhattan, you find those Saturday-night-fever blisters made famous by John Travolta: the teen-age dance clubs where every boy dresses like Travolta in a white, trim-line suit, and everybody does the same step in the same style till they break for the tables where they all talk the same "towhk."

These are the dating spots that were stalked by Son of Sam, the Grendel of the disco world. (I was at Studio 54 the night they nailed Sam heading out for a disco in Queens with an automatic rifle in his car. Right in the middle of *Star Wars*, the sound system died as if someone had pulled the plug. The nearly hysterical voice of Steve Rubell, the club's manic owner, blabbered over the PA: "They got Sam!...Son o' Sam!...They *got* 'im!" A mighty cheer rose from the disco floor. The sound system soared again to full volume, preventing the implosion of the walls. As the gleaming planets revolved triumphantly, the tribe celebrated the vanquishment of its most implacable enemy—one of those "bridge and tunnel people" that would never have been allowed through the door.)

The wildest and most revealing discos are those that cater to the rough-trade crowd down on the Hudson River docks, where you find dives with brutally suggestive names that conjure up visions of chains and manacles. These are Mob-protected joints, where you check your coat at the door and swagger around in cowboy chaps with your balls swinging free. Where fourteen-year-old boys dance above the bar in jockey shorts or a crazy masochist douses himself with lighter

dollars a drink charged to enjoy the spectacle of all the other rich Europeans scuffling around on an old-fashioned dance floor that appears to have been left over from the Art Deco thirties. At Infinity, down near SoHo, in a dark, cavernous, turn-of-the-century factory loft decorated with neon halos and phalluses, two thousand kids from the boros, dressed for the boardwalk at Coney Island, writhe and scream and hail each new record dropped on the turntable as if it were an apocalypse. The Paradise Garage, the hottest gay disco, is an immense cast-concrete truck garage fluid and sets his body on fire. These are the discos with the orgy back rooms, where you stick your cock through a hole in the wall and hope for the best. Where the boys bugger each other in chorus lines. Where a hard-muscled, hairy arm with a big fist plunges first into a can of Crisco and then so far up some guy's asshole that his eyes bulge.

The one thing that binds all of these otherwise dissimilar establishments together is the music and the shared atmosphere of overstimulation. If disco is emblematic of where it's all at today, then the stunning profusion of lights, sounds, rhythms, motions, drugs, spectacles, and illusions that comprises the disco ambience must be interpreted as our contemporary formula for pleasure and high times. The essence of the formula is the concentration of extremes. Everything is taken as far as it can be taken; then it is combined with every other extreme to produce the final rape of the human sensorium. Why?

## SPILLED RELIGION

ONE answer is that modern man has so dulled and dimmed his senses by living in an excessively stimulating industrial environment that nothing but sensory overkill can turn him on. Another, more sympathetic, interpretation is that the search for pleasure in the modern world is not motivated by decadent and insatiable hedonism. Quite the contrary, it is a displaced quest for certain spiritual values that can only be attained by breaching the barriers of the senses through overstimulation. What modern man craves most cannot be obtained through moderation. "The path of excess leads to the palace of wisdom," proclaimed William Blake. The kind of wisdom that Blake was thinking about was not the "once burnt, twice cautious" prudence of the self-preservative middle class. He was suggesting the genuine wisdom possessed by the man who can transcend the normal limits of human experience and attain thereby not only a detached and philosophic view of this world but even a glimpse of the mysteries beyond.

Ecstatic enlightenment has always been the implicit goal of our frenzied popular culture. Only the squares, the dummies, the moralists, and the old and dull have ever believed that Jitterbugs were crazy. The great dance fads that rise like tidal waves once every decade and that sweep across our country like crusades are continuations and reminders of our intensely religious heritage. When the Puritans founded this country, they severed the sacred from the secular and set the stage for what some regard as the excesses of religious mania and what others view

as the fitful flourishing of the divine fire. As the hold of established religion has weakened and died, the craving for some sort of primitive religious enthusiasm and rapture has remained just as strong today as it was in the days of the southern gospel churches or their predecessor, the Great Revival, when the worshippers at the round-the-clock camp meetings would become so aroused by the ceaseless chanting, singing, and preaching that they would quake and shake uncontrollably, roll upon the ground, go into trances, and speak in tongues. Such spontaneous outbursts of popular and primitive religious feeling are by no means solely American. You find them even more powerfully exemplified in the Carnival at Rio and the Brazilian and Haitian voodoo ceremonies, in the dancing sickness of the Middle Ages, and so back through history until you come to the twin fountains of European civilization, the Greeks and the Hebrews—the former with their Dionysiac cults and crazed bacchantes; the latter with their ecstatic dancing before the ark of the covenant or around the golden calf. The truth is that throughout the history of Western civilization there has always been a buried life, an underground tradition of primitive tribal religious rites and ecstasies that burst out periodically in epidemic manias that puzzle the learned and lead the moralistic and the despairing to postulate the decline and fall of the West.

The discomania of our day is just such another outburst of chorybantic ecstasy. Like all its frantic ancestors, from the Charleston and the Lindy to the Twist and the Boogaloo, the disco scene is a classic case of spilled religion, of seeking to obtain the spiritual exaltation of the sacred world by intensifying the pleasures of the secular. What differentiates disco from its predecessors is its overt tendency to break all the bounds of conventional morality and spill over into orgy, as it did first in the gay world. All disco is implicitly orgy: The question is whether this steadily mounting impulse is carrying us toward the natural fulfillment of our long-repressed but recently liberated sexuality and sensuality or whether it is a signal that our souls are dying and we are reverting to the condition of animals. Orgiastic encounters can be animalistic and degrading or decadent and debauching or violent and destructive. But they can also be drastic devices for fulfilling and stilling the clamor of the senses and the obsessions of the mind so that the soul, especially its most religious organ, the imagination, can focus on the ultimate vistas of the spiritual world. By offering the instant and total gratification of all sensual desires in an atmosphere of delirious excitement, the orgy may promote the dawning of an exalted state of consciousness, of *extasis* or, literally, standing outside the body. In this exalted state, we experience the full force of the higher energies of the universe, which otherwise teem down upon us with as little effect as the fabled influences of the stars.

Since this view of disco differs so drastically from the conventional wisdom, I have sought to give it a firm foundation by composing the first full-length portrait of this hitherto slighted phenomenon. I realize that I am claiming a great deal for a form of entertainment that has always been regarded as a fad, a folly, a brightly colored bubble about to burst. But I intend to trace it up from its roots, associate it at each phase in its history with the cultural climate it reflected, and analyze the aesthetic elements of music, dance, and theater that have gradually evolved and coalesced to produce the modern discotheque. What follows may be read as the jerky and jagged fever chart of the latest outbreak of the dancing sickness; or, as I believe, it may be seen as the often baffling, sometimes sordid, but ever-renewed quest for ecstasy and transcendence.

*Cave in St.
Germain-des-Près*

## IN THE BEGINNING

N the beginning was the word—and not much else. *La discothèque* was a coinage, a neologism, in a language that traditionally has resented and rejected such novelties. Formed by analogy with the French term for library, *la bibliothèque*, a discotheque meant a record library. The word implied nothing about dancing, and when it appeared first in the thirties, along with *discophile* (record lover), it applied usually to collections of classical recordings. The first place of public entertainment to employ the word as its title was a bar, La Discothèque, in the rue Huchette, where you could order with your drink a performance of your favorite jazz record. Whatever the origin of the word, the origin of the discotheque as an institution is perfectly clear. It was a product of the austerities and prohibitions imposed on wartime Paris by its German conquerers.

The Nazis kept some of Paris's famous entertainment establishments going full blast during the war years because they themselves wanted to enjoy the fabled pleasures of these incomparable restaurants, follies, and brothels. What they would not tolerate was the popular pastime of dancing in public to American-inspired swing bands. Jazz stood with Jewish art at the very summit of that list of proscribed forms that *der Führer* had stigmatized and banned as dread examples of cultural decadence. Indeed, in the most atrocious and alarming examples of debauched art, such as the cabaret operas of Kurt Weill and Bertolt Brecht, there was an obscene mingling of the Jewish and Negro racial strains that suggested among its other horrors the unspeakable defilement of miscegenation. If the decadent and cowardly French wished to submit themselves to the debauching influence of this jungle music, they would do so only at their own peril.

Forced underground, jazz became a symbol of the French Resistance. The foremost French authorities on jazz were forced either to hide their collections of the forbidden records or to camouflage them with other labels. As for public dancing: One could only engage in it on a surreptitious basis. Since there were no dance bands like the ones that had been popular before the war, music for dancing had to be provided by rigging certain *caves* on the Left Bank with crude public address systems that could broadcast whatever records the proprietors felt safe in offering to their clandestine patrons. Disco was born, therefore, in an underground atmosphere that has continued to cling to it up to the present day in the supposedly tolerant and permissive milieu of American society.

## JUKIN'

N America, long before the war commenced, dancing to records in public places had become a familiar pastime. In the South, it was called "juking," an interesting word derived from the Gullah dialect of the sea-island Negroes of Georgia and South Carolina. In Gullah, *juke* or *joog* means "disorderly" or "wicked," just as *jazz*, which is derived from a similar African source, means "sexual intercourse." When

you went out jukin', you spent the night in some raunchy roadhouse dancing to the sounds of that remarkable invention of the thirties, the jukebox.

The jukebox can be traced back to 1899, when the owner of the Palais Royal Saloon in San Francisco installed an electric, motor-driven Edison phonograph. It had four listening tubes, and the machine was activated by inserting a nickel in a slot. But technological drawbacks caused a long hiatus between the invention of the jukebox and its establishment. Prior to the introduction of electric amplification in the late twenties, no phonograph could make enough noise to compete with the clatter of the player piano or the uproar of a mechanical band. So it was not until Repeal (January 5, 1933), when thousands of

taverns, bars, and restaurants reopened, that the box became a familiar feature on the American scene. Once established, it began to have a profound influence not only on the music business but on the aesthetic sensibilities of the American public.

For years, every Saturday night, the top ten tunes in the country were announced with breath-bating expectancy on *Your Hit Parade*. The rating was dictated exclusively by that week's jukebox play. Even the magic number, ten, reflects the influence of the box, which originally could play only ten records.

During the war, the era of *Jukebox Saturday Night*, the boxes played twenty-four hours a day as factories adopted swing shifts and the lonely,

spaced-out workers took their 4:00 A.M. breaks in cafeterias devoid of any other form of amusement. By war's end, the machines were utterly worn out and a massive effort was needed to replace them.

The swing bands broke up in the wake of the war, and there has not since been any large-scale revival of dancing to live orchestras. Instead, for the past thirty years there has been a steady growth of disco dance. Though the French improvised the institution out of necessity — like onion soup — they took an early lead in refining it into an art — also like onion soup. The first innovation after the war was a distinctive nightclub package that was invented by Paul Pacine. He dubbed his new formula, Whiskey à Go-Go.

*Malt-shop*
*bobby-soxers*

## WHISKEY DISCO

THE first Whiskey opened in 1947. It was designed to exploit the eternal French obsession with *le jazz hot* and the new taste for Scotch whiskey. "Go, man, go!" was the ritual shout of the "hep cat." Whiskey was an exotic drink in a nation of wine bibbers. The most amusing feature of the new nightclub package was the decor. Taking his theme literally, Pacine decorated his clubs with brilliant tartans and covered at least one wall with lids of whiskey cases emblazoned with those evocative names: Ballantine's, Dewar's, Johnny Walker, MacGregor, Cutty Sark, and Haig & Haig. Within a decade, every major city and resort in Europe had a Whiskey.

Meantime, in Paris, the most popular discotheque became Chez Castel, located on the rue Princesse in St. Germain-des-Près. A typical evening of the period would commence with a movie, show, or concert; then, after the theater, one would go for supper to La Coupole, the huge, old railroad station of a restaurant located in Montparnasse. La Coupole, a landmark establishment left over from the twenties, was flanked by the Dom and the Select, a couple of cafés familiar from the pages of Hemingway. The restaurant stayed open nearly twenty-four hours a day and could service three to five hundred diners at a sitting. The atmosphere of the place was always very Bohemian, with artists like Giacomotti and writers and intellectuals like Jean-Paul Sartre and Simone de Beauvoir among the regular clientele. When supper had been concluded, about one o'clock in the morning, the chic way to end the night was to repair to Jean Castel's place, which was just about half a mile away — almost close enough to walk in good weather, if you didn't have a chauffeur and a car.

Chez Castel was operated strictly for the in-crowd; you couldn't even find the place if you didn't know exactly where you were going. No sign appeared on its dark red facade. There was only a little plate with the house number, 15. As far as tourists and strangers were concerned, the watchword was *"Ne passeront pas!"* To the right of the entrance at a grubby bistro bar, Castel himself presided, hailing his affluent customers and kissing the pretty girls like a man throwing a party in his own home. Across the ground-floor hall was a little kitchen with a few dining tables. Upstairs was a formal dining room decorated in the elegant style of *la belle époque*. The discotheque was, as always, in the cellar, which had been transformed into an ornate jewel box in fake tortoiseshell, plush, gilt, and mirror glass. There was barely enough light to see the dance floor, a tiny checkerboard of copper and steel tiles. The idea of the midget floor was one that went back to the original supper clubs of the twenties and thirties. The floor was a space saver; but more importantly it promoted a feeling of closeness and intimacy—of bodies brushing lightly against each other—that was considered romantic in the days of dancing cheek to cheek.

Castel was a shrewd operator and he made the most of all those things that have always characterized discos; but, oddly enough, what gave the place its final kick was not the club but its next-door neighbor, a greengrocer, who opened very early in the morning. Instead of rounding off the night by making the traditional pilgrimage to Les Halles and eating onion soup while ogling the *types*, the new thing was to enter the greengrocer's shop at dawn, dressed in furs and evening clothes, and browse through boxes of damp produce picking out bunches of watercress, radishes, and leeks.

## ENTER RÉGINE

IN the year 1960, Castel discovered that he had a formidable rival in the recently opened Chez Régine. The now-famous proprietor of this club had worked her way up through the ranks of the discotheque business by starting out a decade before as an attendant in the *pipi*, or ladies room, of the Whiskey à Go-Go. The daughter of a Polish-Jewish refugee named Joseph Zylberberg ("a known criminal of marriages and breaking up of marriages," who ran a little bar called the Lumières de Belleville), Ré-

at the Serviceman's Canteen with actresses like Katherine Cornell and Shirley Booth. After the war, he became the MC of the Palladium Ballroom and presided over the Mambo era. During the '60s he achieved fame as America's foremost dancing master, giving demonstrations, lessons, and organizing Twist contests. Subsiding into retirement only after a serious illness, he still holds forth at the Friar's club after forty years of hot dogging across America.

*Twist contest*

Twist was launched by the black kids in the ghetto. It was part of a group dance called the Madison. Chubby Checker, a nineteen-year-old singer from Philadelphia, picked up the routine and began touring the country with it, singing a song called *Do the Twist* that had been recorded in 1959 by Hank Ballard. Though Checker was a great promoter of the dance, what pushed the Twist over the line from the ghetto into the heart of white America was the same force that rocketed Régine to fame: the Jet Set. The setting for this epoch-making event was a sleazy Times Square bar called the Peppermint Lounge.

A rough and raunchy hangout for sailors,

*Joey Dee*

Once the Twist was picked up by the media, its fame spread across the world with epidemic velocity. Twist records and Twist movies and Twist experts popped up everywhere to turn on all the people who hadn't been on a dance floor in years. Eventually, there wasn't a finished basement or a living room in the United States that hadn't seen some of the same action that had immortalized the Peppermint Lounge.

Why did the Twist get everybody into such a lather? Apart from such obvious reasons as its compulsive rhythm and the simplicity of its execution, the Twist was an explosion of the Afro-American subculture that has fueled practically all of the dance crazes of the twentieth century. Dancing is for special occasions in suburbia, but in the ghetto most any time will do. Dancing all the time does the same thing to dance steps as it does to a pair of shoes: It wears them out. Black people are the trendiest of all people (except gays), and they've always got to have something new to step off on. There are just so many expressions possible in the vocabulary of black dance; so what happens typically is that some old-time step or rhythm is revived, slicked up, and launched as

leather-clad bikers, and hookers with beehive hairdos and toreador pants, the Peppermint looked like a set for *Grease*. When the house band, called the Starlighters and fronted by a twenty-two-year-old singer named Joey Dee, would go into its Twist numbers, the waitresses, who wore tight short aprons over slacks, would slam down their trays and shimmy onto the floor to give the boys a good time.

Somehow the joint was discovered by the Beautiful People, whose slumming parties were soon picked up and broadcast by Oleg Cassini, the gossip columnist whose pen name is Cholly Knickerbocker. Overnight, the Lounge became the hottest spot in New York. Into its plastic interior poured the likes of Greta Garbo, Noel Coward, Elsa Maxwell, Tennessee Williams, the Duke of Bedford, and the Countess Bernadotte. The celebrities were followed by the press, the photographers, and the trendy people. Soon the door had to be manned by five tough-looking bouncers. The original customers were condemned to sit at the curb gunning their motorcycles in frustration because it was impossible to get into the place.

the latest thing. Hence, when you review the history of black dance in America, you get the impression of an endless recycling of steps and struts that usually go all the way back to the years when black people in this country were first getting their heads up and their acts out in front of the public — the enormously fruitful years just before and after World War I. The Twist provides a perfect illustration of the whole process.

The step itself is an ancient move that goes all the way back to the earliest black minstrel and medicine shows. Jelly Roll Morton, the king of New Orleans piano players, sang a song around the turn of the century about "sis . . . out on the levee doin' the double Twis'." Just before World War II, another black piano man, Perry Bradford, wrote a song called *Messin' Around* that explains how to do the step:

> Now anyone can learn the knack.
> Put your hands on your hips and
>   bend your back.
> Stand in one spot, nice and light,
> Twist around with all your might.
> Messin' round, they call that
>   messin' round.

Later still, the step was incorporated in yet another dance routine called *Ballin' the Jack*. It was used by blues singers between the verses of their songs and by Lindy Hoppers during the break in the dance where the partners split to do their own things.

The African quality of the Twist is unmistakable. The rotation of the buttocks, the focal point of African body culture, and the bent-leg squatting posture, which draws the dancer down toward the earth instead of allowing him to rise above it as in the European dance tradition, are typical of every Afro-American dance from the Shimmy to the Black Bottom to the Samba. For white middle-class Americans, who are always locking themselves up in the straitjacket of a culture that admires the body but is ashamed of the ass, the thrill of the Afro dances is exactly the same as the thrill of sexual liberation. With the Twist, America learned how to "get down."

All the other characteristics of the Twist are just as African as the movements — from the sundered state of the partners to the trancelike state of mind it induces. Dancing in primitive

societies is a tribal act. Instead of pairing off, the dancers merge with their group. All the earliest Afro-American dances, like the Ring Shout, were group dances; and when black people were cooped up in the big-city ghetto, they continued to dance in the same compact masses at rent parties and in black ballrooms. All night long the music would continue without a break, just as it does in Africa; but instead of a line of drummers thundering out the beats, the urban blacks would grind and shuffle to the syncopated rhythms of a boogie-woogie piano professor, whose powerful drive and endless rhythmic variations would make him a one-man band. In America as in Africa, the final effect of the music, the dancing, and the rhythm was to get stoned. The whole disco scene of our day is basically an extension of the old-time rent parties: a classic example of the ghettoing of America.

Once white Americans start dancing, they don't stop for a long time. If they overcome their initial sense of inhibition, they experience an extraordinary sense of release. Every dance craze from the Charleston to the Lindy to the Twist to the Hustle shows the same pattern of social

momentum. The Twist was soon followed by a whole series of new dances: the Slop, the Mashed Potato, the Swim, the Monkey, the Pony, the Bug, the Frug, the Hitchhike, the Watusi, the Hully-Gully, the Jerk. Most of these steps were the property of the teen-agers, who were rapidly taking over American culture during the rock days. Eventually, instead of everybody doing the same step in the same style, the pattern exploded into a totally free-form happening.

The first great wave of dancing took place in the same social settings that had seen the Lindy and the Shag, the Truckin' and Peckin' of the previous generation: those sock-hop balls in high school gyms and jukebox Saturday nights in roadside taverns. The funneling of all this wild action into discotheques did not occur until late in the decade. In the year 1960 there weren't any discotheques in America. Or, at least, there weren't until the very last day of that year, when the same people who brought you the dance, brought you the dance hall.

HE Jet Set was the first social clique to employ the discotheque as its rallying point. Analogous to the high society of prewar days in its mixture of American money with European titles, the Jet Set was also the heir of the old café society. Neither traditional society nor café society provides, however, the proper formula for this coterie of immensely influential tycoons, gossip columnists, well-bred beauties, European nobles, and American theater people; their tone was far too democratic for the former, and their power vastly exceeded that of the latter. The Kennedys alone controlled the worlds of international politics *and* fashion, to say nothing of their influence on the arts, on the media, and on modern manners and morals. The French term for the Jet Set is a much better description of the role of these people in contemporary society. *Les locomotifs* is what the Jet Set is called in France, the idea being that wherever the engine pulls, the other cars in the train must follow. Once the locomotives got on the disco track, they were certain to drag the rest of the world along. First, however, these streamlined engines had to be furnished with a Grand Central Station at the hub of the modern world: New York City. Providing this ideally designed terminal was the task of the man who for many years drove the locomotives along their tracks: Olivier Coquelin.

Coquelin was a radically different type from Régine. He was born into the *haute bourgeoisie*, of a family that counted on one side the owner of two of the finest hotels in Paris, the Meurice and the George V, and on the other side, the proprietor of a cork factory that enjoyed a virtual monopoly of the French wine stoppling business. A *bon vivant*, a poet of pleasure, and a man who likes to live at the front, Coquelin began his career in America by joining the army during the Korean War and performing such feats of heroism on the battlefield that he was awarded both the Silver Star and the Bronze Star, as well as a Purple Heart. Granted citizenship for his services to a country that was not his own, Coquelin returned after his discharge to his family's profession: managing hostelries and entertainment establishments. He spent three years making Sugarbush in Vermont the country's premier skiing facility; then he decided that he had had enough fresh air for a lifetime. Enough tropical sunshine, too ("Palm Beach," he remarks, with characteristic disdain, "is not a place — it's a season"). He recognized that the social world was dominated now by the Jet Set, and established for the Beautiful People a discotheque on the Upper East Side of Manhattan that would provide a welcome alternative to the stale, old-fashioned atmosphere of the Stork and El Morocco. "The best, the ideal place," he reasoned, "would be a nightclub where you could find the most beautiful girls and sit next to a man and talk about anything and everything your heart desires — except sex and money." So was conceived the idea for Le Club.

### "A FRAYNCH HUNTING LOHDGE OF THE SAVAHNTEENTH SAINTUREE"

**L**E Club. What a perfect name! How appropriate that a French institution borrowed by the capital of the English-speaking world should be designated by an English word borrowed by the French language and pronounced either *à la Française* or *à l'Anglaise*, according to the speaker's nationality or personal preference. What's more, the place was a club in the oldest and strictest sense of the term: purely private, with a board of governors, initiation fees, annual dues, and a very clubby atmosphere. If you wanted to sum up the cosmopolitan and international character of the Jet Set, its passion for Europe and its blasé attitude toward the sources of its own wealth and power in provincial America, its sense of exclusivity and self-sufficiency and its determination to enjoy the pleasures and amenities of the Old World while making the most of the excitements and incitements of the farthest-out metropolis of the New World, you could hardly do better

than that snobbish little monosyllable. To this day, the phrase "Le Club" strikes a native New Yorker's ear like an arch little tap on his cheek by a lady's fan.

As for the character of the place, it was a product of happenstance mixed with careful reflection. The building at 416 East 55th Street in swank Sutton Place was originally a garage next door to the apartment house in which Coquelin lived. Its only occupant was a lingerie photographer to whom Coquelin made an offer he couldn't refuse: one hundred free dinners over a period of two years. The backers, who raised the relatively modest sum of $85,000, included men like Michael Butler and Igor Cassini (who had been associated with Coquelin in the development of Sugarbush) and such luminaries of the Jet Set as Henry Ford and the Duke of Bedford.

When Coquelin called in his architect, Pierre Scapular, to give him the specifications for the room, he demonstrated that he was a man who knew his own mind—and his own business. Speaking in his intriguing accent, which he has never lost, he told the astonished architect that his commission was to create "a Fraynch hunting lohdge of the savahnteenth sainturee." If this notion sounds a trifle recherché, keep in mind

$12.00
MINIMUM PER PERSON

that the creator of Le Club had spent many years knurling to fine focus his mental image of the ideal social setting. In fact, like a number of disco operators in the years that followed, he conceived of the room primarily as a personal habitation designed to fulfill his own tastes and life-style. To put it bluntly, Le Club was a French playboy's dream of the ultimate seduction pad. (All of Coquelin's subsequent establishments have been romantically moody, fantastic bachelor lairs, from the underwater cave of L'Ondine to the Anglo-Indian officer's club of Hippopotamus to the ultimate fantasy of Habitation Le clerc in Haiti, a James Bond daydream of Caribbean *luxe, calme et volupté*.) As practical as he was visionary, Coquelin reasoned that "eef wharse came to wharse, Aih would haave at leest a magneeficent apahrtement in wheech Aih maight leeve or raint as Aih pleezed." Ah, the French! So refined, so materialistic—and so shrewd!

Le Club still stands, still prospers, and is still decorated precisely as it was twenty years ago. The approach is down a typical East Side residential block — blank, quiet, enlivened only by an occasional dog walker. The entrance to the club is so small and inconspicuous that it is easily missed. When you step through the door, endorsed with a little plate reading "For members only," you step into another world, another century. The bar is wood paneled, low ceilinged, and decorated with eighteenth-century Italian allegorical figures in gauzy draperies. From this cozy nutshell, one

LE CLUB
NEW YORK

EL5-5520

CLOSE COVER BEFORE STRIKING

gazes into the main salon, a capacious two-story room of perfect proportions, hung on one side with a huge seventeenth-century Belgian tapestry of the crowning of the Queen of Sheba and answered on the opposite wall with a Louis XV brown marble fireplace, with a couple of comfortable sofas pulled up before its blaze. Hunting trophies, old weapons, and musical instruments mounted on walls of terra cotta pink, plus an imposing crystal luster, complete the decor. Most of the floor is covered by elegantly set tables with floral centerpieces, glass-shaded candles, and fine linen. As in the discotheques of Paris, the dance floor is so small and inconspicuous, tucked discreetly under the grand tapestry and flanked with two small loudspeakers, that one could gaze at the room for minutes without noticing it.

Le Club was anybody's idea of "class"; the great question was whether it would have "pizazz." Assuming the French cuisine would be excellent, the service worthy of the great tradition of *cuisinerie*, the guest list studded with noble titles and celebrity monickers, there was still the distinct possibility that the club would bomb. The test came on opening night, which was New Year's Eve, 1960.

The society girls were delighted by the host's good taste and found the ladies' room especially kicky: On the vanity was a one-gallon jug of Arpège secured to the table by a gold-link chain. The men were impressed by the clubby atmosphere and the wine list. The plan of entertainment was to start the evening off on a low key by playing the then-fashionable continental music (which had taken hold in America thanks to the currently popular French and Italian films), then escalate gradually to more and more lively strains till the belles and beaux were doing the Twist. Everything went according to plan and the opening was adjudged a success; but Coquelin was deeply aggrieved by the music, which instead of describing a smooth arc of mounting excitement, started and stopped, faltered and fumferred, as if the *discaire* hadn't the faintest idea of what he was doing. In fact, he hadn't.

America's first disco DJ was a very pleasant and deferential black gentleman named Slim Hyatt. He had been recruited for the club by society bandleader Peter Duchin. Coquelin had asked his friend Peter for an unemployed musician to spin the discs. Duchin had replied: "I have

just the man you want." When everything went wrong on opening night, Coquelin called Hyatt on the carpet. "What sort of instrumaint do you play?" he demanded. "As a matter of fact, I don't play any," confessed the embarrassed Hyatt. "Then you are a *dansair*?" queried Coquelin. Again the reply was in the negative. "A *singair*?" persisted the perplexed proprietor. "No, sir," replied Hyatt. "As a matter of fact, I am Mr. Duchin's butler. You see, he didn't have the money to pay me jes now, so he said I should take this job." Coquelin hit the ceiling; but after he had tried a couple of real musicians with uniformly dismal results, he went back to Hyatt and gradually trained him in the old French art of spinning.

Like all discotheque operators, Coquelin's policy was "take the cash and let the credit go." The initiation fee for Le Club was only $150 and the annual dues $35. Many of his wealthy and famous patrons were accustomed to signing for everything they purchased. Coquelin would not permit anyone to put a drink or a meal on the tab. One night his maître d' came to him and whispered that Henry Ford had just signed his dinner bill. "Tell him he must pay in cash," ordered Coquelin. "But his name is Ford!" exclaimed the perturbed functionaire. Coquelin strolled to the great industrialist's table and assuming his most charming manner, he explained that the rule of the club forbade dining on credit. Ford smiled and said that he would be happy to pay in cash but he never carried any money. Coquelin replied that he would be just as happy to lend one of the world's wealthiest men fifty bucks.

As the fortunes of Le Club waxed through its first year of operation, troubles of various kinds began to crop up. The biggest problem was the disco's location. Though Sutton Place was fine for such an elegant establishment, the neighbors were outraged by the traffic, the noise of the music, and especially by the patrons' high jinks, which sometimes spilled out onto the street. It was alleged that one dashing young Jet Setter had obliged his tipsy date by driving his car up over the curb to the door of the club. Another night, one of the society girls amused herself by riding up and down the street on the hood of a car. On yet another occasion, Coquelin himself got into a violent altercation with his friend and associate, Gigi Cassini. The two well-dressed gentlemen had a punch-up on the sidewalk at 4:00 A.M. Soon protests were pouring into all the appropriate city agencies. Meantime, the angriest neighbors took to pelting the distinguished habitués of Le Club with eggs.

On one never-to-be-forgotten evening, the Duke and Duchess of Windsor arrived at the club, accompanied by George Plimpton and Ava Gardner. The Duke, as Coquelin recalls, "waz moving a leetle from saide to saide." As the Duchess turned to enter the club, an egg came flying down from a neighboring building and burst on the Duke's elegant monogrammed slipper. As the quondam King of England stared uncomprehendingly at his shoe, which had turned a bright shade of chrome yellow, the horrified Coquelin hustled his guests inside. The Duke was so astounded that he stood riveted to the spot. As he puzzled numbly over the incredible transformation that had been wrought on his slipper, the Duchess rounded on him angrily and snapped: "Why are you standing there when you have been told to come in? When you're told to move, *move!*"

Eventually, the tensions generated by the first and most refined of all American discotheques produced a conflict among the membership, and Coquelin resigned his position in the interests of harmony. His departure from Le Club did not signal any retreat from his ambition to domesticate the discotheque in America—quite the con-

trary. Within a few years he had opened Ondine several blocks away, near the Queensboro Bridge; and over the course of the next fifteen years, he developed many more discotheques, including two, the Hippopotamus and Cachaça, that are still going strong in the same neighborhood. Meantime, New York City was becoming the center of the disco world, with hundreds if not thousands of discotheques springing up—not one of which could ever match for elegance and charm Coquelin's seventeenth-century hunting lodge.

The next few discotheques established in New York continued to exploit the tradition of the chic, exclusive, and exotically decorated Parisian *boîte*. Geoffrey Leeds created L'Interdit ("The Forbidden") in the cellar of the Gotham Hotel—the same location is occupied today by L'Oubliette ("The Dungeon"). This club became the hangout of the younger socialites, who dubbed it "The Sandbox." A far more successful and durable discotheque was Shepheard's, in the Drake Hotel, which Leeds designed to conjure up the atmosphere of the famous house of intrigue in Cairo. In 1964, Joseph Tankoos opened a private discotheque called Il Mio Club in the Hotel Delmonico (where Régine's is located now), whose designer, Pini di San Miniato, sought to evoke the famous Grotta Azzurra in Capri. The disco was equipped with a fountain, "to give the guests the sound and feeling of swimming." Its social secretary was a Hungarian countess and its board of governors included Don Gonzalo de Bourbon, Frederick E. Guest II, and Prince Alexander Hohenlohe. This hoity-toity establishment marked the end of the continental phase in New York discotheques; within a year of its opening, the typical New York disco featured near-naked girls squirming in cages suspended from the ceiling and doing the Frug.

## ROCKY PARNASSUS

**W**HILE disco in the sixties was functioning as the playground of the Jet Set in Paris, St. Tropez, and New York, in London it became the throne room for an entirely different social elite — the charismatic figures of the rapidly burgeoning Pop Society. Revitalized by the powerful creative energies of the Beatles, the Stones, and the Who, the London of those years was transformed suddenly from the decaying capital of a vanished empire to the pop capital of the world. Swinging London was a dizzy whirl of fashion photographers, models, hairdressers, film actors, journalists, and modish rockers. At the very center of this social vortex stood an extremely exclusive discotheque which, from its clubby atmosphere and baronial decor, suggested nothing so much as the Jet Set's hunting lodge in Sutton Place. The name of this interesting establishment was the Ad Lib.

The club was suspended high above the city, in a penthouse in Soho. You entered by squeezing into a tiny elevator which was filled with the music that was being played in the club. When you stepped out of the car and into the drawing room of what had once been a very posh apartment, you were struck by the view over the Thames and by the bizarrely clad company of Carnaby Street Irregulars. The best image of the club and its society is brought to imaginary focus in that marvelous picture book *Rock Dreams*, the hagiography of rock. At the middle of the volume is an imposing two-page spread that shows the whole pop court assembled to pay homage to their Serene Highnesses, the Beatles.

You behold on the broad, murallike photo-canvas a somber but richly bedight drawing room centered on a marble fireplace and hung with a crystal chandelier. The gleaming parquet floor is carelessly strewn with floriated Persian rugs; the furniture is Louis XV. One wall is pierced by an extensive picture window through which glimmers a breathtaking view of London Bridge and the lights of the city. Carefully arranged within this impressive chamber, with its dark oak paneling and classical pilasters, are a score of noble rockers dressed in Edwardian costumes and gathered in casual groupings. Ringo and John are at the center of the canvas; Paul and George stand at either side. Posed about them singly or in clusters, either sitting or standing, some in profile, some full face, are the courtiers: Keith Richard, Anita Pallenberg, Brian Jones, Jeff Beck, Keith Relf of the Yardbirds, Patti Boyd, Scott Walker of the Walker Brothers, Alan Price, Eric Burdon, Keith Moon, Charlie Watts, Mick Jagger, Marianne Faithfull, P. J. Proby, Sandie Shaw, Zoot Money, and Georgie Fame. Needless to say, no such congress of notables ever convened; but the idea of the Ad Lib as the rock Parnassus is conveyed superbly in this canvas.

The impact of the Ad Lib on the American disco scene of the sixties was far greater than anything that had ever been brought from Paris. The first truly popular disco in the states was directly inspired by the London club, and it would be no exaggeration to say that this first fabulously successful American discotheque set the pattern for everything that followed. The name of this landmark institution? Arthur.

## SYBIL AD LIBS

**A**RTHUR was the brainchild of the most talked-about woman of her day, Sybil Burton. Her notoriety was entirely a product of public outrage over her divorce, after fourteen years of marriage and two children, by Richard Burton, who was intent on marrying Elizabeth Taylor. In those days of marriage *über alles*, nothing could incite the ladies of America more than the thought of this poor, jilted wife and mother, who had given the best years of her life to a man who was notorious for his drinking and wenching. The fact that Mrs. Burton reacted to her divorce by going out in the world and having herself a marvelous time never made the slightest impression on either the press or the women who read about her sad plight as they sat under their hair dryers. If Sybil Burton had wanted her revenge on both the media and the self-righteous

# ARTHUR
## EATS

EGG & BACON CROQUETTES, FRESH TOMATO SAUCE & FRENCH BREAD  2.50

SCOTCH SALMON, THIN BROWN BREAD, BUTTER, LEMON, CAPERS  6.50

HAMBURGER  2.50

ARTHUR PLATTER, CHICKEN LIVERS WRAPPED IN BACON, SPARE RIBS, SAUSAGE IN PASTRY BLANKET AND MEAT BALLS  FOR TWO  5.00

POTATOE PANCAKES, ARTHUR APPLESAUCE  2.50

WHISTLER'S MOTHER'S SANDWICH  3.00

STEAK SANDWICH, ON FRENCH BREAD  4.50

DEVONSHIRE TEA, ENGLISH SCONES, THICK CREAM & JAM  2.00

WEEKENDS $5

MINIMUM $4

housewives of this country, she couldn't have hit upon a better scheme than becoming the manager of the most extravagantly trendy discotheque in the world — unless it were the even more audacious act of marrying shortly thereafter an extremely handsome rock musician who was fourteen years her junior.

Though she is much too modest to take the credit for her own success, Sybil Burton was not only the creator of the first famous discotheque but for years afterwards was its informing spirit. A remarkably ebullient, self-confident, and witty woman, with a great appetite for fun, Sybil, as the whole world was soon calling her, opened Arthur purely as a lark. In the winter of 1964, while living in London, she had discovered Ad Lib. The club enthralled her with its hard-jamming rockers, and its piped-in music. What appealed most to

this daughter of a Welsh miner was the bravado of young working-class girls who came to kick up their heels. As soon as Sybil got back to New York, she set to work transplanting the Ad Lib to Manhattan. Taking just the opposite tack as that of Oliver Coquelin, who wanted to exclude from his club all but the privileged few, Sybil determined to make her discotheque a playground for all the bright little shopgirls, hairdressers, and fledgling models who were just then emerging as a new urban class. She wanted a public not a private club; a place that would be cheap rather than expensive; an uninhibited milieu that would allow everyone to dress as he pleased and do his thing without concern for the old decorum and pecking order of the traditional nightclub with its battles for the best table, its condescending maître d's, and its carefully rehearsed floor shows.

47

The food and drink were to be English pub style with nothing more impressive than shepherd's pie and shandygaffs. The music would be anything that was right for "jigging around."

The financing and management of the club were handled as cavalierly as every other facet of the undertaking. Having spent her life among British and American theater people, Sybil had a wide range of acquaintances who would cotton to such a scheme. She rallied their enthusiasm and raised eighty thousand dollars by the rafflelike expedient of selling eighty shares at a thousand dollars a throw, sometimes dividing one share four ways so that a quartet of relatively impecunious dancers at the City Ballet, for instance, could become partners in the amateurish enterprise. The shares were bought by the likes of Rex Harrison, Julie Andrews, Leonard Bernstein, Adolph Green, Betty Comden, Mike Nichols, and Lee Remick. (Like a fool, I turned one down!)

When it came to designing the club, which, ironically, was located on the premises long occupied by the now-defunct El Morocco, Sybil sought the advice of Jules Fisher — the lighting designer who eventually conceived the marvelous electrical fireworks of Studio 54 — and planned an installation that would have made history by being the first nightclub to be decorated entirely by projected scenery. The idea was to make all the walls projection screens which would light up with photo-murals programmed to the music or which would project the rave reviews of a Broadway show whose cast was celebrating its opening night. Alas, when it came time to install the two hundred projectors which they had bought from the 1964 World's Fair, it suddenly became obvious that the scheme would so restrict the dance floor that the club would be the best-lit table top in history. So the two hundred projectors had to be sold and the lighting cut back to a dinky grid of colored bulbs blinking on the ceiling. As for the decor, it amounted to little more than some painted panels, which were thought to have a "Mondrianish" appearance. The main room focused on a leftover stage where a rock band would alternate with the canned music. The bar looked like a bar.

The final problem was what to call the club. Discothèques in New York had been titled hitherto to suggest exotic and forbidden plea-

sures. Sybil's club demanded something radically different, something spoofy and jokey. Steven Sondheim suggested that they send up the snobbish Jet Set by calling it "Le Clubfoot." Mike Nichols had a better idea. Why not take a bit out of the Beatles' movie? Remember that scene where the earnest reporter asks George, "What do you call your haircut?" George answers, "Arthur." Wouldn't that say it all? Just call the club *Arthur*.

## THE BRITISH INVASION

THE success of Arthur owed little to deliberate decisions and designs and virtually everything to timing and unconscious promptings. In London, Sybil had discovered the beginnings of a cultural vogue that would shortly come cresting over the Atlantic to crash on our shores like a tidal wave. For 1965 was the year of the British Invasion. The invaders ranged all the way from Vidal Sassoon, with his sculptured haircuts and Beatlish-looking hairdressers, to the Royal Ballet, with Margot Fonteyn and the company's new superstar, Rudolf Nureyev. Between these extremes were ranked the British fashion designers (like Mary Quant), the British fashion photographers (like David Bailey, whose mystique was celebrated later in *Blow-Up*), the new-style British actors (like Terence Stamp and David Hemming), and, of course, the great British rock bands, led by the Stones and the Beatles, whose *Hard Day's Night* set America on its ear. Nothing like this cultural take-over had ever happened before in America. Especially in New York, which had just grown accustomed to regarding itself as the new cultural capital of the world, the effect was stunning. The press went mad. The media were agog. The whole country strained to see what was happening. And there in the thick of it all was Sybil, manning the beachhead that was Arthur.

The opening was in May, a season when all the okay people are fleeing New York for the shore, the mountains, or for Europe. Anyone but Sybil would have been worried about this bad timing. "What do we care?" she asked. "We aren't running this club for the toffs." Another consideration was what she would wear. A young Parson's School fashion student named Joel Schumacher offered to make her a dress. "I don't care about the style," shrugged Sybil. "The only thing that matters is that the frock be fireproof."

Opening night was a classic example of disco timing. When the doors were opened about 9:30, only a few people appeared. Mike Nichols walked in, and sensing a failure, he tried to put a good face on things. "I like it this way," he insisted: "nice and quiet." The quiet was soon broken by

an endless stream of arrivals, including a great number of celebrities, the only people well enough informed to know what was happening. Soon the club looked like a jam-up fashion show. Courrèges bumped into Puccis, miniskirts confronted floor-length gowns, black pants suits pranced by lacy baby dolls. The great moment of the evening arrived when Rudolf Nureyev appeared dressed in a brown Beatles suit and did a mean Twist with Sybil, whose fireproof gown turned out to be a pink sheath with feathered sleeves. The next day, newspapers all over the country showed the first Mrs. Burton flashlit on the crowded floor with open mouth and white bouffant hair, getting it on with the stiff-backed, fist-clenched Russian dancer, whose hair had been styled as a blond Arthur.

As with Le Club, the single biggest problem that surfaced at Arthur was the DJ. The solution was provided by the band, the Wild Ones, who had played at the Peppermint Lounge and been impressed by the personality and flair of one of the club's dancers, a young, blond, high-gain enthusiast named Terry Noel. As a Twist dancer in a candy-striped jacket and straw hat, Terry had whipped up one frenzy. Why not another? An emergency call was sent out to find him and bring him to Arthur. He was discovered in the lobby of the Knickerbocker Hotel, painting the walls as payment for his room. Brought to the club the second night, he cut in on Sybil. As they danced, he denounced the way the records were being spun. "It's all wrong," he told the lady, who was of the same mind. Next night, Terry stepped into the booth, and for the first time in America, a discotheque fell under the spell of a really gifted DJ.

Up to this time, the disco sound had been the Paris–St. Tropez style that had been introduced at Le Club and had spread to the other little chi-chi clubs that had opened in Manhattan. First you'd get a French ballad and then a faster American soul tune; then an Italian ballad and another swinging soul sound. The music was continuous but there was no attempt to really mix the records so that the sequence of tunes built to a climax. Far from being charged-up show-biz babies, the spinners were technicians, tucked out of sight in concealed booths from which they peered onto the dance floor through a slit in the wall.

**T**ERRY Noel changed all that. He was in touch with the wild modern music that had come in with rock and Motown. He was a manic cheerleader type, who aimed to drive the dancers through the ceiling. As the Wild Ones, whose game was playing the hits exactly as they sounded on the records, would wind up their set, Terry would come in on the last beat with the recorded version of the tune. Then, he would start to mix the sides so that they built in a steady crescendo. The mix was totally eclectic: It ranged from Frank Sinatra to Bob Dylan to Otis Redding to The Mamas and the Papas. Amidst the familiar standards, he would sling ringers that nobody had ever heard before. One of the first DJs to concentrate on "breaking" new records, he was soon working through hundreds of new sides every week seeking fresh material.

Terry soon developed that empathy with the crowd which is the whole knack of jockeying records. "I felt up the audience," he recalled recently. "There's a feeling the crowd emanates. It's like an unconscious grapevine. They send you a signal and then you talk back to them through the records. When I played a record, the record that followed would make a comment on the record that came before. At the same time, I would never lose a beat or break a rhythm. I'd throw on a Frank Sinatra and pack the floor. I didn't want to play Frank Sinatra, but I knew I'd get them up there with Sinatra. Then I'd go to the Mamas and Papas. Within ten minutes, I'd have them going crazy. I drove to a climax, just like in a play."

Getting people up to dance was one part of the job. Getting them back to their seats again to order drinks was the other part. "My job is to sell booze, to make money for the club; that's why I was paid so much. So I'm driving them to their seats. They're ordering drinks because they're hearing a slow ballad. By the time they've got their drinks ordered, I'm starting up again. I didn't even play the whole ballad. They don't know that. But now that they're relaxing and

getting a little conversation going, I'm driving them up again. They've left their drinks on the tables, and they're back on the dance floor again, enjoying what they're doing. Nowadays, nobody has a table or a waiter. Charge 'em at the door and that's it!"

Getting a DJ who saw himself as an artist meant a club owner could get burned by flashes of temperament. Jazzmen jest bitterly about the drunken asshole who comes weaving up the bandstand and croaks: "Hey boys, play *Melancholy Baby*?" Your switched-on disco DJ is just as outraged by "requests." One night John Wayne

turned up at Arthur and demanded that Terry play a certain tune. However the Duke hits you on the screen, person-to-person he comes on like Mr. Big. When he demanded that Terry spin a certain side (probably *God Bless America*), he got exactly what he deserved. "Is this the record you want, Mr. Wayne," said Terry deferentially, whipping the disc out of the rack. "Yeah, play that," said the actor. With a snap of the wrist, Terry broke the record in half. "Uh, it's broken," he apologized. "I guess I won't be able to play it."

When the management shut off Terry's drinks one night, he deliberately "lost his floor." The

manager, staring into the void, flipped out. Rushing over to the booth, he demanded, "What's going on, Terry? Why isn't anyone dancing?" Terry said, "Murray, would you like to see somebody dance?" "Of course I'd like to see somebody dance," snapped the irate manager. "Well, you see this glass?" taunted Terry. "It's got Coca-Cola in it. I understand that I can't get a drink." "Well," fumferred the manager, "you've been drinking too much...uh...we can't afford it." "Well," sneered Terry, "I can't afford to have anybody dance." With that, he turned the record on the turntable up to ear-splitting volume. Then he turned it down again. "You want to see them dance?" he teased. "Okay, watch!" With that, he flipped another record on the second turntable and flicked the needle across it. "Zhhhhhhp!" went the flying needle till it settled into a groove. Then, as the music poured out of the speakers, the people suddenly rose to go on the floor. "Give him a drink!" cried the defeated manager to a passing waiter.

Terry's other bag was playing the lights along with the music. Though he had nothing more than a ceiling full of colored bulbs, he soon discovered that there were just as many secrets to switching lights as there were to spinning sides. "I found that the heavy combination was between a green and red with a quick flash of yellow in between. In other words, if I was flashing green-red-green-red-yellow-green-red, the more I got green in, the more they would go ape." A few years later, he put his knowledge of colored lights in an old ballroom that Trude Heller bought on Broadway. "It was right across the street from the Winter Garden (a lousy location!). We ripped everything out and painted the room black. There were six square pillars on the dance floor. I put a red, yellow, blue, and green spotlight shining up on each side of the pole. Then, I put adjustable mirrors on top of each pole and mirrors on the bottom. Then I put a smoke machine in the middle of the room. I would create this huge maze of crisscrossed lights, with hexagons, parallelograms—I can't even tell you what—but red, yellow, blue, green beams would shoot up through the smoke. Flashing these lights, especially the green—forget the red—would drive everybody bananas!" Lights, even more than music, would become the next great obsession of disco.

*Terry Noel (far left).*

**51**

## MÉLANGE
## À DISCO

**I**N the meantime, Arthur was broadcasting the disco idea across America. The club had become the focus of pop society in New York. Every celebrity of the day Frugged on its desperately crowded floor, and some of them struggled to articulate the experience. Danny Kaye reported that one night he screamed at the top of his lungs—what lungs!—and no one turned his head. Eli Wallach said, "It's like being stuck in a tunnel with all the horns blowing." Judy Garland, worried about losing her voice shouting over the din, spoke to her date in sign language. Mervyn LeRoy asked a waiter how he tolerated the noise. The waiter replied by extracting from his ears two rubber plugs.

The social mix was as staggering as the sound. Wilt Chamberlin, seven-foot-two, danced beside Eddie Arcaro, five-foot-four. The *premiers danseurs* of the Royal Ballet, the City Ballet, and the Bolshoi did the Monkey and the Jerk with Brooklyn bimbos who danced all day in vinyl miniskirts in the mod windows of Paraphernalia. Playboys in sweatshirts saluted society matrons wearing costly designer gowns. One night Mrs. Paul Roebling appeared in a simple little shift with eighty-eight karats of diamonds worth $950,000 hanging from her ears. For Sybil the most extraordinary visitor of all was Princess Margaret, who had never before been inside a discotheque. The Welsh miner's daughter, after a warning call, received the royal princess with her escort of Secret Service men at the door. The Princess withdrew to a banquette and stared, fascinated, all night at the floor. Asked what was the oddest step she had seen, she replied: "Sybil's curtsey."

As with Studio 54—which Arthur prefigured in countless ways—rumors were rampant that the club was controlled by the Mob. Violence did erupt on more than one occasion. The most notorious incident was a shooting that occurred

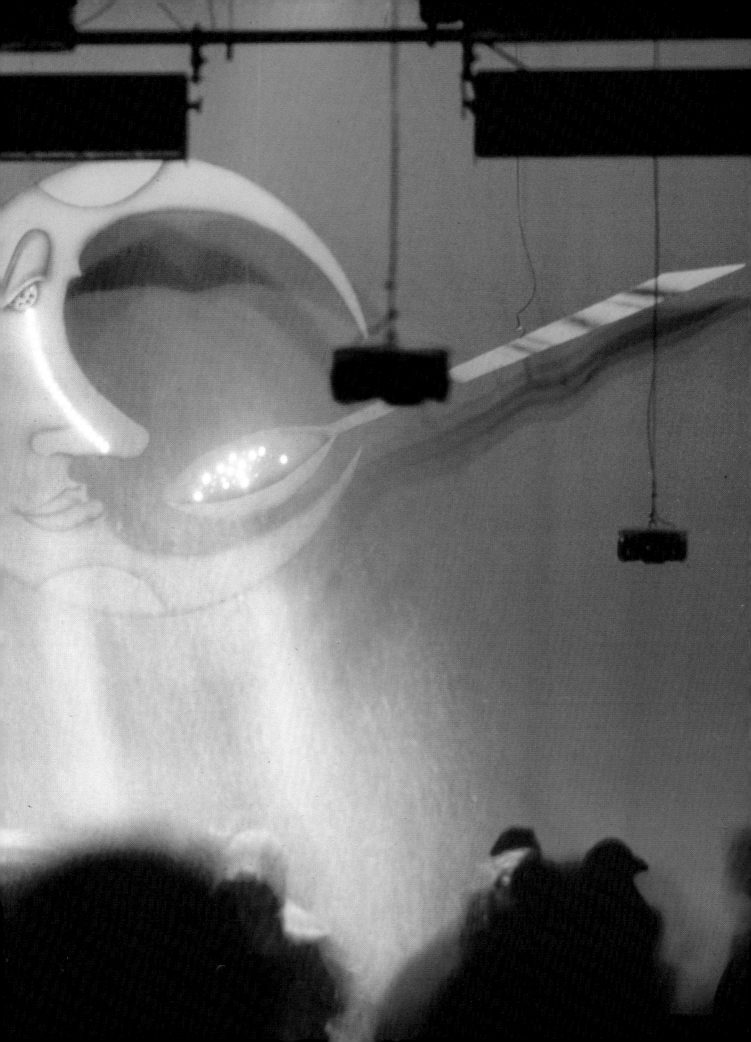

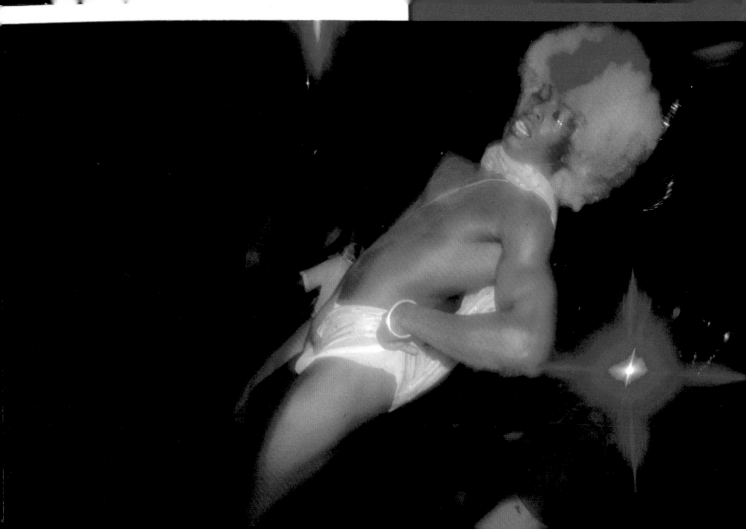

BANDERILLERO BOOGIE

Sixth Floor NYC. 1974

Ice Palace 1975: Fire Island

LE CLUB
NEW YORK

XENON

The Gallery

18
82Ω

Moskowitz    25

©SONIA

STUDIO 54

phyllis diller +
David Brenner

George Burns    82Ω

82Ω

Dotson
Truma

a Ross at
o 54    6

35    Peter Frampton +
Elton John    17

82Ω    Xenon

grace jo
Hurrahs

NIA MOSKOWITZ 1978    13

28 MO

ART GARFUNKLE

REDIT TO
SKOWITZ

D28

Carroll,
Ea
Kitt
82Ω

26  28
MOSKOWITZ 1978

REGINE

2

ON

e Jones —
Mouches

Lillian Carter at
Jaipur Ball-Studio 54

STOCKARD CHANNING
ALLEN CARR —
"GREASE"

SONIA MOSKOWITZ 1978

SONIA MOSKOWITZ    9+

Roberta Flack
Ahmet Ertegun
Jerry Hall, David Frost

Xenon
SONIA MOSKOWITZ

Kir
81-8

OSMO
NEW Yo

2

OSKOWITZ    840ζ    8+

Sonia

TZ 1978

D28

Norman Mailer

studio 54

couple a

studio 5

Sonia Moskowitz
Di ... tally - studio 54 +

Olivia Newton-John + Ryan Can

SONIA MOSKOWITZ 1978

D28

Studio 54

Margaux Heming

Studio 54

PLEASE CREDIT TO
SONIA MOSKOWITZ

D28
15

Regines
Telly Savalas + son

Dolly Parton

Bjorn Borg at studio
54

D28

STUDIO 54

Karl Lagerf

STUDIO 54

Gypsies "
- Regine's

S. Moskowitz

7/25/78
YORK

Moskowitz

D29 Xenon

Sonia Moskowitz

John-John Jr + sister?
studio 54

SONIA Moskowitz

Gilda Radn

D28

XE NON

x 3ξ EO Woody Allen

MUHAMMED ALI

30

PLATZER

30- RP

Kodak

8ξ

PROCESSED BY KODAK

X CHER

Mick, Bianca and Halston

"ITALIAN"

ole Shields o
and
friend

ROBIN PLATZER

J. T.

30

30. B
LIZA

PLAT

STUDIO 54

Barbara Carrera +
Potassa

Issey

Diane

D28-S.M

JACKIE BIS...

liyake

eeland

to OLIVIA

Margaret Trudeau

Tom Sullivan

WONA MOSKOWITZ

HALSTON

Kodak

Studio 54

PEEL THAT
WHEEL

**The full-face photo of Grace Jones** by Sonia Moskowitz is a black and white to which the star applied exactly the same makeup that she wears onstage.

**Disco Orgy** by Robin Platzer.

**Pink Record I:** Man in the Moon by Neal Slavin.
Insets: left, top to bottom, by Steve Cooper, Jeff Tennyson, Russell Turiak; right by Ron Lieberman, Sonia Moskowitz.

**Pink Record II:** left by Edo; right by Allan Tannenbaum.
Insets: left, top to bottom, by Sonia Moskowitz, Robin Platzer; right by Sonia Moskowitz; bottom two by Russell Turiak.

**Pink Record III:** all photos by Jeff Tennyson.

**Pink Record IV:** Man with Cigarette by Bobby Miller.
Insets: left by Bob Deutsch; top right by Bobby Miller; all others by Sonia Moskowitz.

**Studio 54** by Roxanne Lowit.

**Banderillero Boogie** by Paramount Pictures.

**Le Club** by Christopher Makos.
Inset courtesy of Larry Silverman.

**Low Note** by Russell Turiak.

**Xenon** by Allan Tannenbaum.
Inset by Neal Slavin.

**Peel that Wheel** by Ian Patrick.

**Fisheye photo** by Christopher Makos.

cushion-strewn crash pad, where bands would jam and kids would dance until they dropped and passed out. The most obviously exploitable element in this unique and highly perishable environment was the light show, which had become a conspicuous feature of the place. It consisted of projections of free-form patterns that were obtained by mixing oils on plates and then blowing up the amoeba-shaped colored blobs on screens above the bandstand. With the blobs slowly oozing before the crowd's besotted eyes and a handful of photographer's strobes cutting the murk into silhouetted snapshots, your well-stoned hippie could well believe that he was experiencing ecstasy.

The first East Coast attempt to cash in on this hippiedrome idea was the Cheetah, a huge, sprawling discotheque on Broadway in the Theater District, constructed in the old Arcadia Ballroom and owned by—of all people—Olivier Coquelin. The sophisticated Frenchman had come a long way since the days of Le Club. In the interim, he had opened a rock disco called L'Ondine, which was decorated with fishnets and other aquatic props. For a season, he had also opened and operated one of the many new discos that had sprung up on Long Island to cater to the summer beach crowd. The year Cheetah opened, this Southampton disco named after Coquelin's favorite sea delicacy, L'Oursin ("Sea Urchin"), had

changed hands and been taken over by a much more trendy group. The new owners hired a young lighting wizard named Richard Goldstein, who had installed a fascinating *son et lumière* spectacle called Lightworks. It was at L'Oursin sometime in the course of a whirling, festive Labor Day weekend in 1966, on a night that blended the moods of midsummer night's eve and Halloween, that I got my first taste of this extraordinary new type of entertainment.

Pushing into the murky interior of the club, I found my way to a table. Then, after attuning my senses to the stunning mélange of sights and sounds coming from every direction, I made a snap decision to remain there for the rest of my life. Never had I beheld such an intriguing spectacle. A huge dark hollow with giant images flashing on its walls, with dancers in summer whites flitting about like ghosts, with rock music so powerful that it practically sucked you out of your chair, L'Oursin was enthralling.

In the first half hour, I must have regressed about thirty-five years. I was back in the early thirties with my mother on the Steel Pier at Atlantic City, staring at the fox-trotters; I was inside a glamorous speakeasy in Cleveland (the Great Lakes Exposition of 1937) watching a multifaceted glass ball revolve in the ceiling; I was lost at some high school prom in the forties, my ear divided between the hiss of sliding feet and the

nasal sweetness of saxophones. Wow! Did I go back! But after a while the nostalgia began to wear off, and my thoughts took a different turn. "Those dancers out there on the floor, what do they look like? It's the tribe readying itself for an orgy. What is an orgy? It is an alignment with force—like iron particles patterned by magnetic fields. Combine enough excitement with enough narcosis and you slip out of yourself and perform acts of public sex with no embarrassment or guilt. Is it a holy act? Yes, because it celebrates some force greater than the individual's consciousness and outside his consciousness." So spoke my stoned soul.

## A PRE-CHRISTIAN VERNAL RITE

**W**HEN I met Goldstein I asked him about the powerful erotic character of his discotheque. He laughed and said that he had made the same discovery on the very first night he had shown the Lightworks in his loft on Chris-

topher Street. It was Christmas Eve and he decided to combine his love of entertaining with his desire to give his new equipment a trial run; so he invited about seventy people to his house, taking care that they be of different types, from the sophisticated to the naive. By the end of the evening, about half the crowd had left and Goldstein was in the kitchen preparing some coffee. When he came back to the parlor, he found his guests had succumbed completely to the spell of the lights and music. They were all embracing happily, participating in a spontaneous love-in. Goldstein said he was astonished not only by the event but by the gentleness and affection everyone displayed; it was, he said, "a love feast, a pre-Christian vernal rite." At L'Oursin, however, the erotic stimulus had produced some disturbing incidents. One night Goldstein found one of the middle-aged yacht captains exhibiting himself to a group of startled ladies; on another occasion, a whole table rose at the end of *Zorba the Greek* and smashed their glasses against the wall.

Like a lot of people in the pop arts at that time, Goldstein felt he had a redemptory mission; he had discussed the therapeutic uses of lights and music with psychiatrists, and he had discovered the psychic dangers of the discotheque ambience. He said the flashing mechanical strobes used everywhere could trigger an epileptic seizure. He explained that he had no use for the hard-rock line adopted in most discotheques. Instead of giving his audience a flogging, he preferred to provide them with unlimited opportunities for dreaming. Angst, he said, is what spoils hard rock. Dancers don't need this kind of stimulation; users and hippies can get high looking at anything. The emphasis, therefore, ought to be on the values of good showmanship.

Goldstein's gentle disco aesthetic was quickly drowned out by the clamor for more and stranger sensation. By 1967, when the next great discotheque opened in New York City, rock had entered its final freak-out phase. The goal was to push every sensation, every effect to the limits of human endurance. Rock bands appeared before huge ranks of speakers that resembled acoustic firing squads. Rock shows became gladiatorial combats between performers and audiences that sometimes concluded with the kids rushing the stage like lemmings. The foremost rock stars—

Jimi Hendrix, Jim Morrison, and Janis Joplin—offered themselves up to death like fanatical martyrs. The whole of pop culture drifted backwards toward the Stone Age. No institution in the world caught and projected more vividly the spirit of those final days than disco's maddest arena, the Electric Circus.

## CIRCUS MAXIMUS

THE Barnum of the Circus was no hippie. He was a young, good-looking, Brooklyn-born talent agent at William Morris named Jerry Brandt. A representative of top rock bands and a talent scout, Brandt kept his door open to all sorts of weirdos. One day a guy showed up who was a wig salesman. He offered Brandt a pathetic little demo record which was quickly rejected. Then the dude reached into the bag in which he carried his wigs and fished out a crude-looking scrapbook. It resembled something a grade-school kid would paste together as his class project. When Brandt opened the cover, his eye was caught by the phrase, the "Electric Circus."

The rest was a childishly written proposal by a fifteen-year-old kid in San Francisco to put together a circus that would travel across America putting on free shows in the hippie spirit.

There was something about this book that captured Brandt's imagination. He kept it by his side for weeks, showing it to people and wondering why it obsessed him. Gradually, an idea formed in his mind. The old Peppermint Lounge had closed the year before, yet everywhere people were up on their feet dancing to the latest rock hits. What if he were to put together a way-out, futuristic version of the old Twist joint, with all the latest sounds and sights, interspersed with real circus acts and kooky boutiques selling hippie clothes and doing tattoos? Obviously, the project would cost a lot of money. Clearly, he would have to find some rich backers. Who would they be? Brandt tried one wealthy hustler after another; they all failed to come through with the money. Then one day he found the answer to his financial problem just as accidentally as he had stumbled over the original idea. Reading the financial notices in the *Times,* he spotted an announcement by the Coffee Growers' Association stating that they had a budget of six million dollars to promote the drinking of coffee by teen-agers. Brandt picked up his phone.

Soon he was engaged in prolonged negotiations with the growers. They were Spanish and suspicious. Even when he had sold them on the idea of a discotheque where coffee would be the only beverage, they still expressed grave doubts about his ability to build the "Big Bean." Finally they agreed to give him a letter of credit for $250,000—on condition that he make no use of the letter until he had built his club, mounted his production, and sold the first ticket at the door. Brandt took the letter to a building contractor who began work immediately.

The site of the new venture was an old Polish workingman's club on St. Mark's Place, the hub of East Village otherness. Andy Warhol had converted the upstairs social hall into the Balloon Farm, where he featured his rock band, the Velvet Underground. Several steps below the pavement was an early soul club called the Dom. Ivan Chermayeff, who had designed the American Pavilion at the World's Fair, had the bright idea of gutting the old hall and converting it into a giant tent made of white Hellenca stretch yarn.

In this manner, Jules Fisher's idea of a club whose walls would consist entirely of projection screens was finally realized. The rest of the work—the installation of an enormously powerful sound system, the wiring up of scores of spotlights and projectors, the recruiting and rehearsing of circus acts—was just a matter of hundreds of people working thousands of hours until everyone was virtually insane.

Brandt was a brilliant hype artist (a talent he later exploited to puff a virtually nonexistent rock singer named Jobriath to national prominence without so much as a single record or concert!). Night and day, all the local media intoned the spooky message that the Electric Circus was "the ultimate legal entertainment experience."

On a hot night in June, Brandt fulfilled his promise to the coffee growers. After paying out $330,000, he sold his first ticket. In fact, he sold a great many tickets. Four costumed karate experts passed the customers inside, two at a time, $15 a head, until three thousand people had filed past a sign in the lobby stating: "Occupancy by more than 740 people is illegal." The joint was obviously a gold mine. Though the *Village Voice* compared the Circus with Rome before it fell, a more accurate analogy would have been a skyrocketing stock on the market. As for the show inside, I am fortunate in being able to quote a detailed, though laboriously composed, description by an uptight professor at Columbia University, who was among the first visitors to the new pop shrine. His account appeared alongside some excerpts from a forthcoming novel by Philip Roth, *Portnoy's Complaint,* published in the *New American Review.*

### CAVE OF DREAMS

**Y**OU make your way," wrote Professor Albert Goldman, "through a gaggle of young hippies sprawled on the porch steps, and enter a long, narrow alcove where the faithful, the tourists, and those somewhere in between wait in line for admission in a mood of quiet expectancy, like people waiting to get into one of the more exciting exhibits at the World's Fair. Once inside, the spectator moves along a corridor bathed in ultraviolet light in which every speck of white takes on a lurid glow, climbs a steep staircase and passes through a dark antechamber. Here the young sit packed together on benches and, already initiated into the mysteries beyond, stare back at the newcomer with glazed, indifferent expressions, as though they had been sitting there for days. Then, suddenly, there is a cleft in the wall, and the spectator follows the crowd pressing through it into a gigantic hall that suggests a huge bleached skull. Its dark hollows are pierced by beams of colored light that stain the walls with slowly pulsing patterns and pictures: glowing amoeba shapes, strips of home movies and giant mandalas filled with fluid colors. The scream of a rock singer comes at you, the beat amplified to a deafening blast of sound.

"Housed within this electronic cave are hundreds of dancers, a number of them in exotic, flowing garments, their faces marked with phosphorescent insignia, hands clutching sticks of incense. Some of the dancers are gyrating frantically, as if trying to screw themselves down into the floor; others hold up their fists, ducking and bobbing like sparring partners; others wrench their heads and thrust out their hands as if to ward off evil spirits. For all its futuristic magic, the dance hall brings to mind those great painted caves, such as Altamira in Spain, where prehistoric man practiced his religious rites by dancing before his animal gods.

"Magnetized by the crowd, impelled by the relentless pounding beat of the music, you are drawn out on the floor. Here there is a feeling of total immersion; you are inside the skull-like cave, inside the mob of dancers, inside the music, which comes from all directions, buffeting the dancers like a powerful surf. Strangest of all, in the midst of this frantic activity, you soon feel supremely alone; and this aloneness produces a giddy sense of freedom, even of exultation. At last

**THE ELECTRIC CIRCUS!
ST MARKS PLACE
EAST VILLAGE. NYC**
The Ultimate Legal Entertainment Experience. Air-Conditioned in more
ways than one. For information: 777-7080. Come. (Stoned)

you are free to move and act and mime the secret motions of your mind. Everywhere about you are people focused deep within themselves, working to bring to the surfaces of their bodies deep-seated erotic fantasies. Their faces are drugged, their heads thrown back, their limbs extended, their bodies dissolving into the arcs of the dance. The erotic intensity becomes so great that you wonder what sustains the frail partition of reserve that prevents the final spilling of this endlessly incited energy.

"If you withdraw from the crowd and climb to the gallery overlooking the dance floor, you soon succumb to the other spell cast by this cave of dreams. Falling into a passive trance, his perceptions heightened perhaps by exhaustion or drugs (no liquor is served here), the spectator can enjoy simultaneously the pleasures of the theater, the movies and the sidewalk café. At the Electric Circus the spectacle of the dancers alternates with the surrealistic acts of professional performers. An immaculate chef on stilts will stride to the center of the floor, where he looms high above the dancers. They gather around him like children, while he entertains them juggling three apples. Then, taking out a knife he slices the fruit and feeds it to his flock. High on a circular platform, a performer dressed to look like a little girl in her nightie struggles ineffectually with a yo-yo. A blinding white strobe light flashes across her body, chopping her absurd actions into the frames of an ancient flickering movie. Another girl comes sliding down a rope; someone dressed as a gorilla seizes her and carries her off with a lurching gait. Sitting in the dark gallery, you watch the crepitating spectacle below. The thumping music sinks slowly through your mind like a narcotic. Eventually, you close your eyes and surrender to the longing for silence, darkness and sleep."

The Electric Circus was a mind-blower and the greatest freak show in New York. The hippies had decreed that every night in the year must be Halloween. At the Circus they arrived in costumes that easily eclipsed anything that had ever been seen under the big top. Yard-high hairdos, thrift-shop collages, Tussaud time-trips, and tattooed-lady body-paint were the order of the day. When these human effigies got out on the dance floor, they resembled the figures on a mechanical clock designed by Salvador Dali.

**103**

**A**CCORDING to the pundits of pop culture, the sixties was the greatest age of dance in the history of America. The problem with the pundits is that most of them aren't old enough to remember anything earlier than rock. Ill-equipped by experience or education to stand back and compare one period with another, they make a lot of erroneous assumptions and conclude that their day represented a summit when in fact it was just one of a series of peaks that reached much higher in earlier times.

When you page back to the last great period of pop dance in America, the Jitterbug era, and you look at the old films, listen to the old music, and read the classic analysis of the scene, *Jazz Dance* by Marshall and Jean Stearns, you soon realize that rock dancing was pretty mediocre stuff—just about right for a bunch of bubble-blowing junior-high kids and totally ridiculous when aped by adults. The problem with rock was its sledgehammer beat. Instead of laying a magic carpet under the dancer's feet and lilting him across the floor in a swinging, syncopated pattern, rock riveted its dancers to one spot and then jerked them around like wire-strung puppets. Rock galvanized people into action, but it never released them into the long, flowing choreographic lines or inspired them to do the fast brilliant footwork that is the hallmark of the hoofer. Instead of prompting dancers to improvise fresh combinations of steps, rock laced everyone into a manic straitjacket. The rhythm and the dancing were so crude and primitive that they turned off most real dancers and virtually ostracized professional dancers. Apart from James Brown—who belongs to soul, not rock—who can you name as a great dancer of that day? Swing fostered the development of a whole galaxy of dance stars, from Fred Astaire to Gene Kelly, from the great black flash acts, like the Berry Brothers and the Nicholas Brothers, to the jazz tap geniuses like Groundhog and Baby Lawrence to the rug-cutting, girl-slinging Lindy Hoppers at the Savoy. Swing was a beat that not only got people up on their feet but made them move their feet and finally swept them off their

feet like men shot from cannons. Rock ground people down as they struggled to twist themselves into the ground.

To the restrictiveness of rock's static and rudimentary rhythm were added the further difficulties created by the way in which the music was packaged and played. The three-minute 45 rpm single is an almost perfect medium for a pop tune. It compels the songwriter to get to the point fast and say whatever is on his mind without boring the listener with a lot of repetitions. If the song is a good one, you can always play it again: That's the right attitude for a listener. A dancer makes a totally different set of demands. He wants to get in a groove and stay there until he has exhausted his invention or his body. The time scale and the momentum of any physical activity is vastly different from the attention span of listening. Years before rock, long experience had demonstrated that dancing requires continuous music that is standardized in time and tempo. The traditional dance bands played twenty-five-minute sets, winding up with a medley that tracked through a whole sequence of tunes at the same tempo.

When social dancing was transferred from the

ballroom to the discotheque, a conflict developed between the character of the recorded music and the natural impetus of the dancers. The discotheques of the sixties were giant jukeboxes. They played nothing but short-winded singles and equally short cuts from albums. Every three minutes one tune would fade and another would come surging out of the speakers signaling a fresh start in a different direction. The first disco DJs struggled to compose this incoherent mélange into a semblance of the old continuity, but the material had been created for an entirely different purpose. What's more, they were stuck with the same demand that controlled top-forty radio: They had to play the hits of the day no matter how they added up. So a spoofy song by the Beatles would flip into a frantic performance by the Four Tops, or the relaxed beat-yo-feet-in-the-Mississippi-mud of Memphis would be transformed abruptly into the screaming tension of the West Coast acid rockers. Jolted and jerked from one powerful track to another, the dancer felt like he was being whiplashed on a fun-house ride.

To launch a new age of dancing—as opposed to just moving—it was necessary to get the public off the bumpy, country road of rock and back onto the superhighway of music especially composed and recorded for dancing. The key to the whole process was the shift that began in the late sixties from the pile-driving thump of rock to the ball-and-sock of soul.

All through the sixties, black music in America had been pursuing a path that was independent of rock. While the Beatles and the Stones, Jefferson Airplane and the Doors held the white youth audience spellbound, these groups never made much headway in the ghetto. For every move the rock bands made on the black and white checkerboard of American pop, the black R & B groups made a countermove. As London and Los Angeles dominated the one market, Detroit and Memphis dominated the other. Nowhere was the basic difference more apparent than on the dance floor. As Mick Jagger remarked recently, no white rockers have ever played music that was as good for dancing as the stuff that was laid down by the black bands. The secret was simple. Though the black drummers would play all the standard rock patterns, they would alter the rhythm slightly to make it swing. The greatest drummers of the era were not the British show-stoppers like Keith Moon and Ginger Baker but the anonymous percussionists of Motown.

Motown continued to provide the basic inspiration for dancing in America down to the early seventies, when the company moved to the West Coast. Then the sound began to peter out and lose its authority. Berry Gordy seemed more intent on making movies than he did on making music. Soul began to seem as trite and predictable as rock. The dancing days were over. The discotheques began to board up their doors. The last dance of the sixties symbolized the exhaustion of the era's fabulous energies. Called the African Twist, it consisted in nothing more than standing stock still with eyes closed, shivering from head to toe, as if in the grip of a deep chill.

The Electric Circus survived till 1970, but Jerry Brandt pulled out the year before after a series of frightening incidents that signaled the metamorphosis of the counterculture into the criminal culture. One day, for example, Abbie Hoffman appeared with a "representative" of the Diggers, the famous hippie commune that had run a soup kitchen in Haight-Ashbury. The Digger looked like an apparition from a horror movie. He was

sheathed in black leather, with a heavy bike chain circling his waist and another one coiled around his wrist. His head was crowned with a Nazi helmet. His mission was to demand ten thousand dollars for "the community." Brandt was enraged, but he was also fearful. One of these dudes had rapped Bill Graham in the mouth with just such a chain. Finally, the Circus master decided to play lion tamer. He leaped up from his desk and pulled the extortionist's helmet down over his eyes. Then he threw the leather-clad bully out of his office.

A couple of weeks later, Brandt arrived at the club one night to discover that it had been invaded by three hundred nonpaying Aliens, the East Coast counterparts of the Hell's Angels. The ringmaster called for his clown—who happened to be the president of the Aliens. A violent argument ensued. "What's the matter? Ain't we people?" the clown pled. Finally, the Aliens retreated. The next night they came back, their numbers swollen to three times their original strength. They had called in their brothers from every neighboring state. Brandt realized that he was licked. The club had made a few million dollars. Now it would become a target for every rip-off artist in the East Village. Selling out to his partner, Brandt watched from the sidelines as the Circus struck its tent.

## LET ME TAKE YOU DOWN

**T**HE terminal year of rock and the counterculture was 1970. Its greatest stars were offing themselves all over the world on drugs; the hippies were drifting back home after their fling in the Wild West; but the final blow was the breakup of the Beatles. What had destroyed rock was the venality of its robber bands and the outlawry of the whole subculture, which had degenerated into sheer anarchy. Like all Children's Crusades, the Rock Generation had created a golden opportunity for the pirates who always lie in wait ready to pounce on new marks. Nowhere was this fact clearer than in the social microcosm of the discotheque.

In New York, the discos were now converted into those evil institutions titled euphemistically "juice bars." All over the city, trashy little teen traps were baited and set to spring on poor dumb kids from the boros, who came into town dressed in their glad rags and bombed out of their minds on "reds" and "Sopors." The days of visionary drugs were over; the time had come to extinguish consciousness with downers. The typical juice joint was a dark hole guarded by some heavy hoods at the door and threaded through with dope dealers selling Seconals and Quaaludes. Nobody really danced any more; they stood in one spot swaying to the beat until they fell over. Once a girl was

*Shag dancers, Madison Square Garden, 1938*

down, six guys might come over and gang-bang her. The crooks who ran the clubs grabbed their money at the door and invested it in the next hole they were driven into by the complaints lodged by the neighbors, the police, and the building and fire inspectors. Racket was the name of the game and the biggest players were the Mob.

Typical of this era was the history of one of its hottest clubs: Salvation. Established in the late sixties down on Sheridan Square in the room that had once housed the legendary jazz club, Café Society, Salvation was run at first by a well-liked disco manager named Bradley Pierce. Bradley had been associated with a lot of discotheques. He

**107**

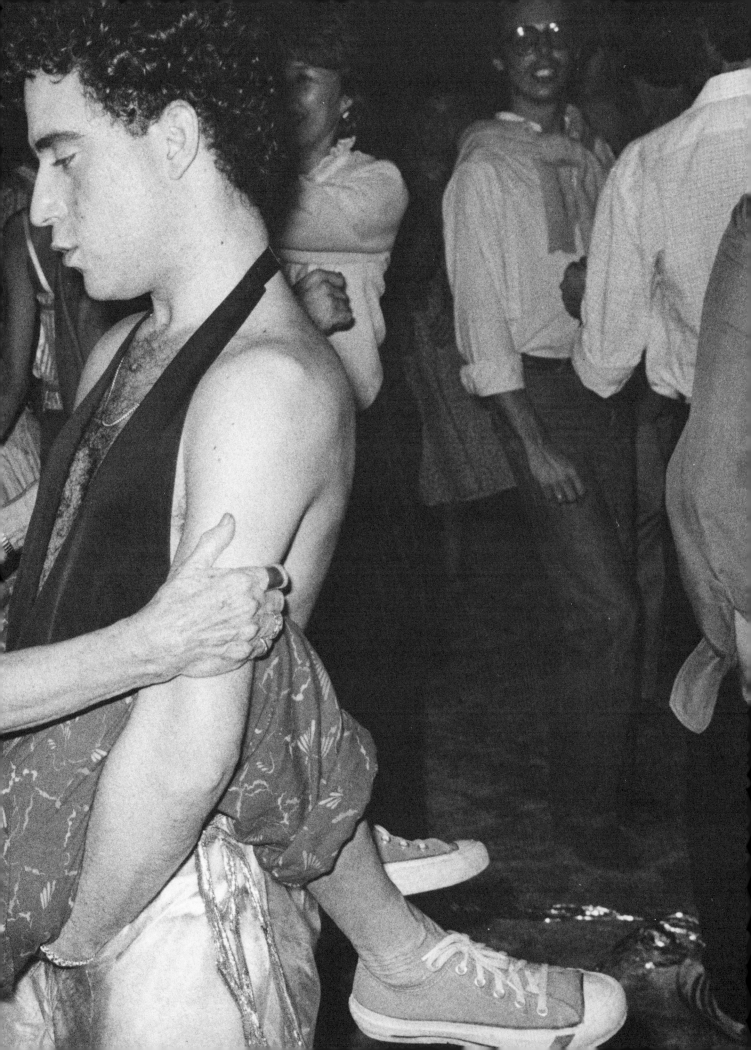

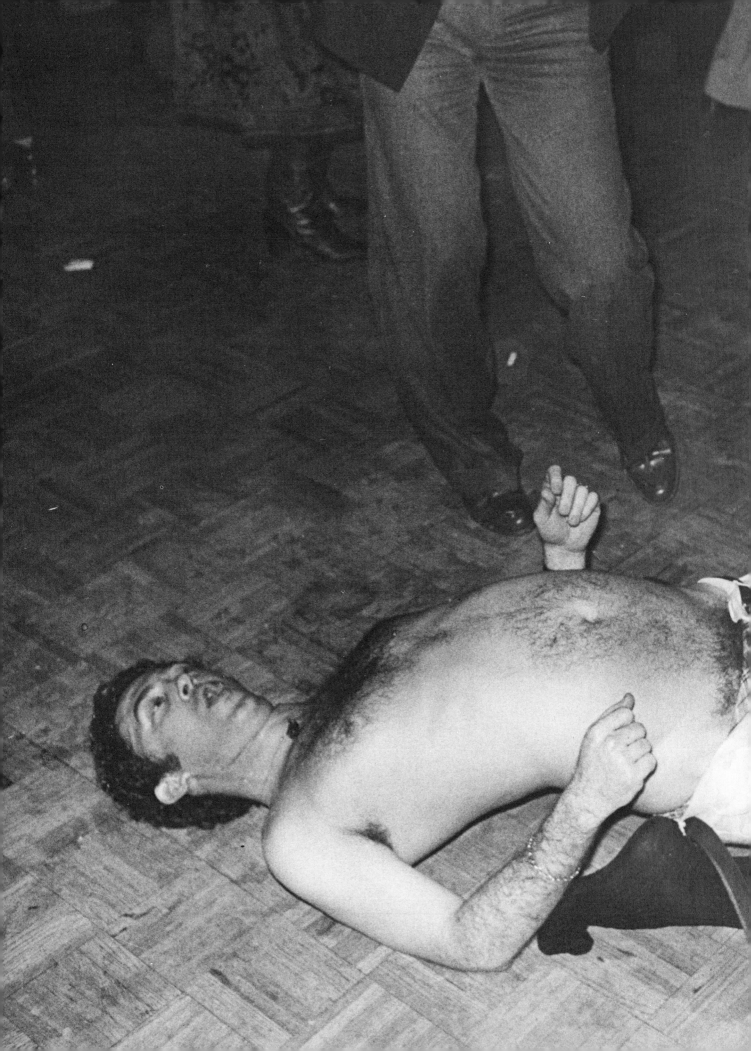

liked to set up a club, make it a success, and then move on to the next challenge. He hired good people like Terry Noel to spin the discs, and he mixed his crowds skillfully.

Bradley's stock-in-trade was his great personal charm. It was said that when a mobster would come into one of his clubs and start waving around his gun, Bradley would take the piece out of the hood's hand, make him laugh, and end up with the killer kissing him. Bradley was skating on thin ice, however; the next guy who took over the club didn't have the same finesse. He cracked the surface and fell through. His name was Bobby Woods. He was a Cadillac dealer from the Bronx who had turned forty, sold his franchise, and was looking around for a hip new life-style. When he bought Salvation, he started wheeling and dealing with the Mob. The club kept losing money and Woods kept offering excuses to the wise guys. One morning Woods was found in a parked car out in Queens. He had been shot four times in the head. His killer was a joker. He had shot the hapless swinger from the four points of a cross.

The juice bars represented the nightmare conclusion of that great counterculture dream of the Street—the place where everybody could get down and get loose and hang out like slum bums sucking on their bottles of Thunderbird. The

other end of the spectrum, the fancy, pampered world of ad-agency geniuses and junked-out rock stars and degenerate scions of hardworking burghers, was just as bad. Here the keynote was sounded by the word *decadence*. In New York all the fashion plates were walking around in crushed velvets and Parisian brothel boots. Their faces were painted up like Toulouse-Lautrec *demimondaines*. They were as languorous as dandies, as jaded as aesthetes, as narcoleptic as absinthe drinkers. Those who could afford it dawdled in luxuriously draped retreats that were filled with the sounds of hidden orchestras, the odors of fuming pastilles, and the shadows of exotic plants cast by motionless candle flames.

When these latter-day Dorian Grays could get their act together, they would repair to some ruinous old movie palace where they could snicker at the antics of Alice Cooper or Elton John: the one, a kohl-eyed queen enacting sick psychodramas with live serpents, straitjackets, mission-oak electric chairs, and guillotines; the other, a corrupt child in a baby-boy boiler suit with a Bozo-the-Clown pin fig-leafed to his fly.

The last dream of the counterculture was to leave both the city and the country and to voyage out to an oasis in North Africa, where the *kef* was plentiful and strong. You would camp there in an ancient Moorish castle until you were reduced to the condition of a zombie: bone thin, flesh numbed, past the thought of thought or even consciousness. If you couldn't take the long trip to Essaouira or Oukaimeden, then you had to search closer to home for something that would send through your jaded sensibility one last tremor of delight. Of such sick dreams was born the most decadent discotheque in history: the Sanctuary.

## HELL'S KITCHEN

**T**HE Sanctuary was located in an old German Baptist church on West 43rd Street between Ninth and Tenth Avenues in what is called Clinton today but was originally and more accurately titled Hell's Kitchen. The disco's

original name was the Church, and its founder, Arnie Lord, had the diabolical idea of decorating it for a Witches' Sabbath. Opposite the altar was a huge mural projecting a terrifying image of the devil, his eyes drawn so that wherever you stood, his baleful orbs were glaring down upon you. Around the Evil One was a flight of angels with exposed genitalia engaging in every known form of sexual intercourse. Before the altar with its broad marble communion table and imposing range of organ pipes stood the long-haired DJ preparing the disco sacrament. With the throw of a switch he could black out the hall and illuminate it eerily with lights shining through the stained-glass windows. His communicants firked around or laid back on the pews, which had been arranged around the walls as banquettes. The bar served drinks from sacred-looking chalices.

Such an outrageous act of desecration was certain to provoke violent protests, even in Hell's Kitchen. From the day the Church opened, the Roman Catholic hierarchy exerted all its influence to have the place shut down. Confronted by the power of the Catholic church, the Church decided to placate its adversaries. The name of the discotheque was changed to the Sanctuary, and the fallen angels' offending parts were festooned with large clusters of plastic grapes.

The Sanctuary had started out as the last word in fashionable folly, drawing a crowd of straight, white celebrities and disco voyeurs, but now it fell into the hands of a very different sort of management. The new churchwarden was named Shelley. He was a flamboyant middle-aged queen who delighted in wearing champagne-colored vestments and great masses of solid gold jewelry, much of it hanging aroung his neck like sommeliers' chains. He sported a great assortment of costly, custom-made wigs, which he kept on display on wooden blocks in his apartment. Shelley soon found himself the owner of the first totally uninhibited homosexual discotheque in America.

Hitherto, the classier sort of gays had congregated at Aux Puces, which attracted a prosperous, fashion-oriented crowd. The Aux Puces was gussied up with a terra-cotta floor, thick carpets, and mirrored walls. Its DJ was named Kathy Dougherty, better known today as Cherry Vanilla. Within a year of its opening, the club changed hands and began the usual slide toward the gutter. When Shelley got control of the Sanctuary, he had a long list of men eager to become members.

A sign of how cool the new owner was about his style of operation was the agreement he made with some Hollywood movie people to allow them to use the Sanctuary as a location for *Klute*, the Jane Fonda film about a New York call girl. Most gay disco owners go through the ceiling when you ask them if you can take pictures of their joints or even mention them in a story. Gay establishments have always protected themselves by drawing a heavy curtain of obscurity over their activities. Not Shelley. He wanted to go Hol-ly-*woood!* He was a lot less happy when the star of the picture demanded that they open the club to women, at least to gay women. Finally, he made the concession of allowing a handful of outrageously dressed fag hags into the club every night.

## PLAY THAT FUNKY MUSIC, WHITE BOY!

NE of the greatest draws at Sanctuary was the only straight guy in the place, its legendary DJ, Francis. The most influential spinner in the short history of the craft, Francis Grasso is a small, muscular, long-haired lad from Brooklyn who got his start in the business working as a dancer at Trude Heller's club in the Village, where he was obliged to perform on a narrow ledge against the wall that allowed him to move only laterally, like a figure in a frieze. One night while visiting Salvation II, a club perched on top of an apartment house on Central Park South (today, the site of the Bengali restaurant, Nirvana), Francis was asked to substitute for Terry Noel, who had failed to show up for work. Grasso approached his trial with fear and trembling; but when Noel appeared, the manager fired him and hired the novice.

Francis soon demonstrated that he had a fresh slant on spinning. Unlike Terry, who was heavy into rock and kept a picture of Elvis Presley stuck up in his booth, Francis worked the soul track. When he got up on the altar at Sanctuary, he would preach that old-time religion with Aretha Franklin, Gladys Knight, Booker T. and the MG's. Into this mix he would drop Chicago's *I'm A Man* and Cat Mother's *Track in A*. Once he had the crowd hooked, he'd dip into his African bag with Olatunji and the authentic Nigerian drums and chants of *Drums of Passion*.

Francis was the first DJ to perfect the current technique for stitching records together in seamless sequences. He invented the trick of "slip-cuing": Holding the disc with his thumb while the turntable whirled beneath insulated by a felt pad, he would locate with an earphone the best spot to make the splice, then release the next side precisely on the beat. When he got Thorens turntables with speed controls, he supplemented his cuing technique with speed changes that enabled him to match up the records perfectly in tempo. He also got into playing around with the equalization controls not only to boost the bass for ass-wagging but to compensate for the loss of highs that occurred when a record was slowed down for mixing. Eventually, Francis became a virtuoso. His tour de force was playing two records simultaneously for as long as two minutes at a stretch. He would super the drum break of *I'm a Man* over the orgasmic moans of Led Zeppelin's *Whole Lotta Love* to make a powerfully erotic mix that anticipated by many years the formula of bass-drum beats and love cries that is now one of the clichés of disco mix.

What this pioneering jock was doing was composing a hitherto nonexistent disco music out of prefab parts. What's more, he was forging the new music right in the heart of the discotheque, with the dancers freaking out in front of him and sending back their waves to his soul, exactly as Lindy dancers used to turn on the jazz musicians in the old swing bands. Not a high-powered show-biz jock like Terry Noel, who wanted to sweep up the audience and carry them off on his trip, Francis was instead like an energy mirror, catching the vibes off the floor and shooting them back again recharged by the powerful sounds of his big horns. Eventually, Francis taught other jocks his tricks and established his style of playing as the new standard.

Once he had become a popular figure in the disco world, Francis was eagerly sought by other club owners. During one of his absences from Sanctuary, he went to work for a tough disco which was full of drug dealers and hoods. One night he surprised some wise guys beating up a dealer in the club's kitchen. They took the peddler's pills and sold them later to the disco's customers. Francis decided that the scene was too rough for him, so he quit and opened his own place in the Village, called Francis.

One night, a man in a business suit stepped into the DJ booth. He told Francis that he had an important message. He wanted to go outside the

FRANCIS FOREVER

club to talk. Francis put a twenty-five minute track on the turntable and followed the stranger upstairs. When they got into the street, the dude turned on him and pulled a gun. Then he led him down the block and shoved him into a waiting car. Francis and his captor were driven by another man around the corner to a dark alley. There he was ordered out of the car and pushed against its side. While the one hood held the gun, the other one cocked up his elbow and, using it as a battering ram, he started smashing it into Francis's face. Working slowly and methodically, the gangster soon flattened the jockey's face to a bloody pulp. Francis went numb from shock. Through the blood that was pouring out of his mouth and nose, he begged, "Kill me...please kill me....I won't be good for anything again!" The hoods had their orders. They had no intention of killing Francis. Their game was maiming him. When they finished their work, they ordered him to walk up the street in the opposite direction from the club. The moment Francis got out of their grip, he made a dash up a wrong-way street. He lost the hit men and made his way back to the club. Before he could staunch the gouts of blood that were pouring from his wounds, the

police appeared. Francis knew that talking could lead to something worse than a beating. He did not file a complaint. It took six months for the swelling of his flattened face to subside. Then it took elaborate plastic surgery to put the broken pieces back together again. When the agony was over, Francis Grasso looked like a different man. But he went back to Sanctuary and continued his career. He's still one of the top jocks in New York.

What happened to Sanctuary's DJ was mild compared with the fate that befell his boss, Shelley. Shelley generally recruited his lovers from the club's waiters, who were chosen in much the same manner as starlets on the old Hollywood casting couch. Often, though, he would leave the club late at night to cruise Times Square, looking for young Puerto Rican boys. He would take the lads home to the sumptuous apartment he maintained near Gramercy Park. The apartment was filled with costly furnishings and chatzkahs. One of his peculiarities was that he kept the price tags on every object in the pad, as if it were a store. This habit, coupled with Shelley's taste in boys, made him an obvious mark. One morning a neighbor found Shelley dead in the bathroom. His skull had been fractured and he had been shot in the chest and stomach. The apartment had been rifled, but the most expensive gold chains and pendants had been left untouched. The thief had assumed, apparently, that stuff this gaudy must be fool's gold.

### HOMO LUDENS

OVER the course of several years, Sanctuary deteriorated from a fancy gay club to a raunchy juice bar. As the tone sank, the business increased, every siren sounding like a seductive song to the thousands of boys who were prowling the city looking for a place to party. The drug dealers who infested all the juice bars made Sanctuary their supermarket. There were so many of them that they could be divided into classes. The two basic types were the low-life dealers and the low-profile dealers. The latter were typically white, dressed like everyone else, and never got caught because they didn't look the type. The lowlifes were the most conspicuous people in the joint.

They were usually Puerto Ricans with names like Chico and Chu-Chu. They dressed in purple, green, and yellow satin shirts, wore lots of rings on their fingers, and were obsessed with shoes. This was the early seventies, when all those clunky, chunky shoes inspired by old comic strips came into style. The dope dealers bought the flashiest, tallest platforms they could find. Their shoes were flecked with silver and shone in the dark as if made of phosphorus. Tottering around on those three-inch lifts, stoned out of their minds, bumping into dancers on the floor, spilling their drugs and wads of money, these schmucks were perfect targets for the undercover narcs. They were always rubbing and scratching their pasty, pimply faces with their long dirty fingernails, scraping off the scabs that formed on their necks and hands from carelessly handled cigarettes.

The pills they were peddling were both ups and downs. Speed was in great demand, but the new thing was heavy downs, especially ludes and the more powerful Paris 400s—blue capsules that had 400 milligrams of methaqualone instead of the 300 milligrams in the standard Rorer 714. Ludes produce an intense sense of euphoria and a tingling feeling all over the body; that's why they're called the "love drug." They also destroy your motor coordination, turning your arms and legs to rubber and making it hard to articulate words. Lude heads are always making jokes about bumping into things ("wall-bangers" is another name for the drug), but you never get the point of the jokes because the speaker is so mush-mouthed that he sounds like an idiot. The Sopor was a lude manufactured in Puerto Rico and sold over the counter in those days. When the ludes ran out, you could always score for reds (Seconals) or tuies (Tuinals), which combined with enough alcohol will put you to sleep—forever.

Drugs were one of the attractions of the Sanctuary; the other was sex. Put fifteen hundred gay boys in a private club, feed them every drug in the pharmacopoeia, turn up the music loud, and pour the drinks like soda pop—presto! You've got an orgy. The rules of the club forbade fucking on the dance floor, although in some straight clubs, such things happened. A girl might get so carried away that she would leap up on her partner, lock her

legs around his waist and bang away to the beat. At Sanctuary you were free to do as you pleased only in the men's room. Every stall was constantly in use as a crib, the cute little angels on the walls staring down on some of the most outrageous behavior that has ever been clocked in a public place.

Francis Grasso, who had become a star by this time, was constantly serviced behind the altar by the fag hags, who were urged on to Olympic feats by the gay boys who admired Francis for his art while despairing of his hopelessly philistine sexual preferences. Francis estimates his tally in this period at about five hundred girls. (Who says being a DJ is a thankless task?) Francis would never permit the ultimate sacrilege, balling on the altar, because that was where his turntables were poised. (Some things are sacred!) He admits, however, to having entertained the thought. "If God was going to strike anyone down," he reasoned, "it would be the people who conceived of this club, not the guys who enjoyed it." With that comforting reflection, he endured three years of this madness.

The dancing at the Sanctuary was just like everything else in this Cathedral of Sodom and

Gomorrah—lewd and lascivious. It was here that the Bump got its start; only it wasn't the cute little hip-hugger, tushie-touching step that it later became in the straight world. It was a frank pantomime of buggery. Two boys could get into it together or twenty could make up a daisy chain. One good bump deserved another and pretty soon the whole room would be acting out its erotic fantasies in the most blatant style imaginable. Bumps led to humps led to licks, shticks, shtups—you name it!

What finally closed the Sanctuary was not so much the licentious crowd inside the club as the spill on the sidewalk. Sanctuary could accommodate at best about fifteen hundred people. Twice that number often collected outside in the street, laughing, shouting, scoring for drugs, and giving each other blow jobs in halls and vestibules. In the summer, when the air-conditioning system failed (as it often did), the huge crowds inside would pour out periodically like the ebb tide, while the masses in the street poured in like the flood. The police hit the joint night after night, but raiding such a mob was not an easy operation. It could take two hours just to empty the club. What's more, as the raids became a nuisance, the patrons became increasingly refractory. When the mild-mannered Francis would announce, "We have to close up now," hundreds of voices from the floor would chorus: *"Fuck you! Let the cops carry us out!"* Whether Sanctuary advanced the cause of Gay Liberation or set it back, the fact is that this discotheque was one of the first places in America where gay militancy raised its clenched fist.

The end came in April 1972. The police and fire departments staged a combined raid. The whole block was filled with flashing fire engines and paddy wagons. The captain in command of the task force presented a complaint that listed seventy-eight separate charges. When Francis walked out of the club that night and surveyed the scene, he flashed: "Gee, this is the first light show I've ever seen in the street!" The doors of Sanctuary were barred for the last time. Ironically, the church was used next as a Methadone clinic.

Disco in New York now rhymed with "homo." The gay boys with their unquenchable lust for lust and their vast amounts of "discretionary income" were the trade that the owners courted. The next well-known discotheque in the city

picked up where Sanctuary had left off. Le Jardin was just a few blocks away on West 43rd Street in the seedy Diplomat Hotel. On the *Tonight Show*, Truman Capote described the scene to a smirking Johnny Carson: "It has these Art Deco couches all along the room, these palm fronds drooping down everywhere, and out on the dance floor, this terrible churning, the whole place churning, like a buttermilk machine." Perfect. Ed McCormack described the curds: "One muscular young madman sports a leather aviator's cap, smoked Captain Midnight goggles and red plastic clothespins clamped onto his bare nipples....The prole decadent generation shake their satin little buns like the swishes of queens, while bellowing as though the testicles of Muddy Waters had been grafted where their tonsils should be." Churn, churn, churn! Churn of fools!

## DISCO À LOFT

**T**HE outrageous happenings of the early seventies made disco a dirty word in New York City. They also persuaded a lot of people to stay home. One of these shut-ins was a sensitive young designer named David Mancuso, who has the bearded, intently staring face of a born zealot. Mancuso was fascinated by the possibilities of the disco ambience; but he realized that to make a disco function perfectly, it would have to be run like a party in your own home. You would have to have complete control over the guest list, firm rules about drugs and sex, and a decisive say about what music was played and how it was put together. Mancuso's home was an old factory loft on lower Broadway near Bleecker Street. It was divided into separate living and working spaces, but it would accommodate lots of people. With good sound equipment and inexpensive decorations and refreshments, it could be made to serve once a week as a discotheque. After some unsuccessful early experiments, Mancuso found the formula he was seeking and soon the most admired disco in New York was a private pad called the Loft.

As will be apparent to the reader, Mancuso's idea was not completely original. Richard Goldstein had been doing much the same thing during the sixties and had furnished his pad with a much more elaborate—perhaps too elaborate—set of light and sound devices. What made the Loft a legend was the composition of the crowd and the extraordinary manner in which its shy, somewhat withdrawn young tenant could marshal the music and play upon the extraordinary collection of people who became his regular guests. The core of the crowd was personal friends of Mancuso, who held numbered cards that entitled them to admission with a specified number of friends.

As the years wore on, the Mancuso circle widened steadily, until it included thousands of people not only in New York but in other cities as well. Though these people were widely scattered, they constituted a tight network. Once, when Mancuso had to cancel a party because of trouble with the authorities, twenty phone calls proved sufficient to spread the word to a few thousand potential visitors. Many of the regulars regarded Mancuso as a saint and a Samaritan. They were highly protective of him and made him into a cult figure. At the same time, Mancuso picked up his share of enemies, who accused him of "playing Christ."

Mancuso's parties were nothing special as regards provisions or preparations. The door charge was four or five dollars. No alcohol was sold or served on the premises. The refreshments were the usual hippie bird food: nuts, fruits, cookies, and juices. The decor was that of a child's birthday party: a ceiling crowded with brightly colored balloons and paper streamers. Instead of the psychedelic fun house of the hippies, this disco was an industrial crucible for melting down races and faces and fusing them into a new society of hard-core disco addicts. Though all kinds of people showed up, 60 percent of the regulars were black and Puerto Rican, an unusual mixture for New York. When Saturday night would roll around and all the public clubs would shut down, hundreds of boys, all steamed up and ready to romp, would converge on the Loft.

The moment you hit the room, your nostrils were distended by the stench of black sweat. The dancers were mostly men stripped down to the skimpiest work clothes and wringing wet. Many of the scruffy boys from the East Village hadn't washed or run a comb through their hair in weeks. On a hot summer night in the un–air-conditioned loft, a visible cloud of steam, of human effluvia, hung over the floor and misted the lights. (At the Ice Palace at Fire Island, which had a Mylar ceiling, this steam would rise, condense, and fall on the dancers like rain.)

The infrared rays that were broiling all this dark meat were ultrahigh frequencies, sounds that reached up into the canine register. Showering down like needles from the hi-fi speakers, they made the old brick walls of the loft ring and zing. This ear-raping effect even had a name: DJs called it "the gay sound."

As the music made the room rock, the boys would heighten the din by banging tambourines or blowing shrill traffic whistles and shouting at the top of their lungs. When the speakers blared *Love Is the Message,* the boys would sing along; only they didn't sing the namby-pamby words of the original. They chanted the classic gay line of the guy who has picked some trashy little fag out of the gutter, taken him home, screwed him and then ended the evening by yelling, *"Throw the motherfucker out!"*

At this moment, perhaps, all the lights would go out. Then, it was ass-grabbing time. When the lights came on again, the dancing was even more furious. Nobody had ever seen such dancing before, such a total human explosion. Even professional dancers were made to feel like dowdy old spinsters, frozen out by the fire of these incestuously excited boys.

Mancuso's house parties revitalized the decadent disco scene, sending a powerful jolt of erotic energy through the human conductors who then transmitted it to the outside world. No wonder people would journey to New York from all over the country just to spend a night in this glowing furnace. The parties also established a new ideal type for the disco dancer. Instead of being a bizarrely dressed fashion fraud or stoned-out kid stumbling all over himself, the new image was the wild, way-out Puerto Rican gay boy, who worked all week as a stock boy at Bloomingdale's or as a hack driver who did the night shift. Though the parties attracted people of all sorts, including a few personifications of intellect like Susan Sontag, their power was generated by precisely those people who were commonly regarded as social pariahs and outcasts, members of that element that most New Yorkers scorned, derided, and were always threatening to ship back "to the jungle." As if in conscious mockery of the stigma they bore, these boys embraced jungle music. One of their favorite tunes was *Wild Safari* by Barrabas, an unknown Spanish band that had been discovered in Europe by one of Mancuso's guests and first played at these parties (where you could buy a copy for six bucks).

Mancuso spun his own discs, and though he was not a great technician, he enjoyed the enormous advantage of being able to play anything he pleased. His tastes were broad and his approach was experimental. He was searching for a new disco sound, a new mix. He wanted to trip people out, to lay them under a spell. Many people regarded him as a magician. His problem was that he was a little ahead of his time. The work he did, however, decisively altered the course of disco's evolution and set it on the path that has led directly to the modern discotheque. Soon other people copied his ideas and opened other downtown loft discos. Nikki Siano, an outstanding DJ, launched his Gallery very easily—he passed out flyers one summer just before the Loft closed. The Gallery became the next hot downtown disco.

## A BROTHERLY LOVE

AT this time, the distinctive sound of disco was the Philly Sound which was radically different from Motown. Instead of the frenzy of *Seven Rooms of Gloom* or the dark, spooky streets of *Runaway Child, Runnin' Wild,* the Philly Sound suggested a new innocence, a new joy, a feeling that everything was coming up daisies. If this appears paradoxical in light of the social conditions of the early seventies, with the

*Kenny Gamble*

chill winds of recession blowing through the ghetto, it should be remembered that pop music in America had always obeyed the rule that hard times beget high times. Some of the gayest, most cheerful and joyous music ever produced in this country was spawned during the Depression. Call it the longing to escape, the flight from reality, the effort to keep the drowning man's head up. The fact is that the instinctive reaction of American music and entertainment when confronted with crisis and despair is to start singing *Happy Days Are Here Again*. Hope was the message of Philadelphia, and love and cheer.

This breezy attitude encouraged its listeners to lay back, cool out and take it easy. What else was there to do? The war in the Nam, the hustler in the White House, the digit at the Unemployment — did anybody really think that songs could change those things? Black people had gone through a lot of heavy changes in the sixties, and where did they end up—back on relief! So the best bet was to turn your back on the jive world

that calls itself the real world and concentrate on being mellow. Saturday was always coming and then it would be time to party hearty!

As party music, as dance music, the Philly Sound was the best sound that anybody had heard in years. It evolved through the big hits of the O'Jays *(I Love Music)*, the Three Degrees *(Dirty Ole Man)*, the Intruders *(I'll Always Love My Mama)*, and the new black national anthem *T.S.O.P.* (The Sound of Philadelphia) which became the theme of *Soul Train*. It made dance music king again. What dancers wanted was a beat that would make their asses swing and a musical atmosphere that would make them feel like they were high on tea. All the other stuff you could keep, because who would pay any attention to it out on the floor? Philadelphia International was right on the money. Repeating the success of Motown, it became America's fifth largest black corporation (current gross: $25 million annually).

It took a while for the new gospel to sink in; all through the early seventies black-oriented pop labels continued to grind out dumb rehashes of the styles established and exhausted by James Brown, Aretha Franklin, and the other big guns of soul. Gettin' down and gettin' funky had become such reflexive acts that nobody could believe that they were as dated as yesterday's newspaper. Until the disco style snapped into focus finally in 1975, the only man outside of the charmed circle of Philadelphia who displayed any real sense of where the culture was drifting was the preposterous but prescient Barry White.

## PIMP TALK

*Leon Huff*

**T**HE Velveteen Hippo, who compounded black bullshit with Hollywood hype so successfully that he became one of the wealthiest singers in the business, is often said to be one of the founding fathers of the current disco sound. The notion does him too much credit. What can be said is that as early as 1973, when he uncorked his classic serenade for astro-strings and cricket, *Love's Theme* (isn't that rhythmic twitch I hear out of my left speaker a cricket?), the Honey Bear understood that black people were a

**121**

lot less interested in funk than they were in glamour. In the ghetto, in those days, the look was Pimp. Now, any dude who walks around in a plum-colored, cut-velvet evening suit, with a frilly white jabot cascading from his breast and a fortune in hot rocks glinting from his fingers; any hammer who tools through the garbage-strewn streets at 4:00 A.M. in an immaculate Superfly pimpmobile, with lightning-bolt side windows, canvas-covered spare tires slotted into the front fenders, fancy chrome scrollwork scribbled on the hood and leather upholstery so fine that it makes you feel like you slipped inside an expensive ladies' purse; any cat or kittie, any stud or stallion who's struttin' around with a couple hundred dollars' worth of Eyetalian-crafted calf on his pedal extremities and a Mississippi gambler or a Bahama planter or a Borsalino Gangster on his konk don't wanna heah no shit 'bout *gittin' down or gittin' funky.* Fuck funk! Funky is jes' wha' whitey wants niggers to be so's he can git his tight little nuts off! Big Brother White was right. The new style was Hol-ly-*woood!*

THOUGH disco had finally found the right groove for dancing, one great problem remained unsolved: The new music the jocks were spinning was still squeezed into the grooves of the old-fashioned 45 rpm doughnut. The restrictions of this short-winded device have been noted before. What most people no longer realize or remember is that the 45 was not developed or adopted because it was an ideal medium for pop music. Rather, it was the patented product of a giant record company that shoved it down everyone's throats back at the time when the long-playing record was introduced in 1948. In those days, the American record industry was dominated by RCA and divided between RCA and its smaller rival, Columbia. The LP was the invention of a Columbia engineer, Dr. Peter Goldmark. When RCA was confronted with a technological revolution, the first since the introduction of electrical recording twenty years before, its officials demanded from their engineers a Victor LP that could compete successfully with the Columbia product and, hopefully, drive it off the market. The result of their hasty effort was the 45, which was simply a reduction of the standard ten- or twelve-inch 78 rpm to microgroove.

Instead of a symphony or string quartet coming in a big book-shaped album with up to eight 78s inside its sleeves, the new RCA package was a little square box with a stack of 45s. You were supposed to buy a $20 Mickey Mouse changer from your friendly neighborhood record dealer that would convert your phonograph into a 45 player. Then you would be right back where you started, hearing the music suddenly interrupted every three or four minutes as the next disc slipped down the spindle.

The idea was preposterous and doomed to failure. The twelve-inch LP was so vastly superior to the RCA product that it was just a matter of time—not much time, incidentally—until it became the industry standard. In that time, however, the two big corporations sat down at the conference table and worked out their differences in the spirit of "free enterprise." It was decided

restrictions, nothing really changed. Half a century of cutting pop music into three-minute lengths had had an absolutely mesmerizing effect on musicians. It was no longer a case of what records would hold: Songwriters couldn't *think* except in three-minute lengths. Eventually, some rock bands began to experiment with longer cuts, and the old habits of mind began to weaken. Still, the market dictated that if you wanted to get your song recorded and distributed fast, you had to squeeze it onto a 45.

*TOP JOCKS:*
*Bobby Guttadaro*
*Tom Savarese*
*Tom Moulton*

When the new age of dancing began and the need to keep the beat going all night long had the DJs jumping from side to side in their booths like fast-food countermen, some guys started experimenting with tape as a solution to the problem. You could sit at home with a Revox and a stack of 45s stitching together a night's entertainment with never a bad segue. What's more, you could sell the tapes to photographers, who wanted to

turn on their models (and then ball them on the darkroom counter) or ship them out to the Sandpiper at Fire Island Pines (where they would drive the gay boys up the walls and then out onto the dunes, where they would roll down to the seaside through a paddle wheel of hands, lips, fingers, fists, and dicks). You could roll up a disco on a reel of tape, but, frankly, it wasn't the greatest.

It was just like those clubs where they wanted to put you inside a glass booth, like an Eichmann. The booths protected you from the idiots who would reach up with a joint in their hands and knock your tone-arm all to hell; but they cut you off from the feedback from the crowd, the vital cues the dancers' bodies sent back to the DJ with voiceless messages. Any DJ worth his Gucci shoulderbag wanted to stay on top of his floor, feeling the vibes and shouting back his answers to the dancers with his next side. The ideal thing would be to have some records that were made for the job. Not these crappy little 45s that lasted no longer than a popper and sounded so horrible when blown up to the volume of a discotheque. These crudely stamped teen toys pushed hi-fi back to the days of cactus needles. What was needed was a special *disco disc,* a custom pressing that stretched the standard three-minute arrangement to five, ten, or fifteen minutes and delivered the music with at least a semblance of the fantastic sound the recordings had when they were played back off the twenty-four tracks of the studio tape recorders.

It took years and years till the record companies got the message. Then they began to receive reports of weird doings in the record stores. Take this crazy *Soul Makoosa* thing, for example. Sometime in 1973, a DJ named Alfie (DJs were even then on a first-name basis like hairdressers) reached into a record bin one day and fished out this little 45 with a grabby title. He gave it a spin and freaked out at what he heard. A soprano sax, blown by some freak in Johannesburg or Capetown, cookin' like a muthafuckah! Alfie told all the other DJ's about this wild African record he had discovered. Everybody made a copy of the disc and soon it was gassing dancers in every downtown disco. When the dancers got their heads together the next afternoon, they began to obsess about this crazy record they heard the night before. They went to their friendly neighborhood record store and bugged the clerk about this *Soul Makusa* or *Macoussa* or *Makoozoo*. Nobody had ever heard of the record. What was this shit? Eventually, the sounds were picked up by some professional musicians, who set to work to "cover" the original. The rip-offs didn't have the authentic flavor of the original. Finally, Ahmet Ertegun and Jerry Wexler at Atlantic got the record and decided to license it for the American market. It was the first of hundreds of such deals that have been made in recent years, as the American record companies have scuffled to pick up on the elusive disco lick. The record finally came out on the American label and sold like crazy. Up and down the grapevine went the word: "Get one of these disco tracks and you'll make a lotta bread, whether or not it gets air play."

The fact was that it would get air play. All the hip radio jocks, like Frankie Crocker, were starting to pick up on the disco scene. They'd go down to the clubs for an evening, pick up a few offbeat sides and spring them on their listeners in odd moments during the tedious traversal of the station's play list. George McCrae's *Rock Your Baby* on the new Miami label, T. K. Disco, had been broken in this way. It wound up as No. 2 on the national charts. Disco was making its point in the world of commercial music. Now, about those special custom pressings....

N 1975, a disco jock named Tom Moulton got the idea of making some special promotion records for his fellow DJs. The records would be specially mixed to extend the length of the tunes, and the pressings would be made on twelve-inch discs, where the grooves would be widely spaced for optimal reproduction. The additional playing time would lighten the jock's work, making them eager to spin the sides and promote the product. At the same time, some enterprising DJs, partially financed by David Mancuso, established the first disco record pool. The pool collected all the new releases from the record companies and distributed them free to jocks, thus reducing the vast amount of time and labor these men were wasting running around from one company to another, collecting the new releases. (Up to this time, most jocks had been spending substantial portions of their meager earnings buying sides at stores like Downstairs Records, a marvelous pop archive located in the subway arcade on 42nd Street and Sixth Avenue.) Stamped "For Disco DJs Only," the new pressings were distributed weeks in ad-

vance of their release date, giving the jocks a chance to build interest in the product before it hit the stores. The idea worked so well that soon dozens of new songs were being auditioned in a Part I/Part II format, with Part II being an instrumental version from which the vocal track (Part I) had been stripped.

The record pirates jumped on these new sides immediately, and soon a lively underground trade was flourishing in bootleg "disco mixes." The next step was as important as it was obvious. One of the new independent labels that had cottoned to the disco sound, Salsoul, decided to market its disco mixes as a new commercial line. The decision was epoch making: For the first time in nearly thirty years, the record industry had a new commercial format, the twelve-inch pop single. Many other companies followed Salsoul's lead. Soon disco fans were enjoying at home the same music they heard in the clubs.

Today you can walk into any record store in New York and find this odd-looking product. It's not in an album designed for one particular record but in a standardized sleeve. It's got a big hole in the center, where the label sticks out, wreathed with a socko logo. The graphic artists have had a ball with this new baby. As you flip through the sides you catch glimpses of kissy, pouty, parted Puerto Rican pink lips (you could get the bends just staring at them!); a black chick and a white chick facing off at each other in thirties airbrush style; or, thick fluid-filled tubular letters; or star-shaped light bulbs studded marquee style; or—well, I'm sure you've seen them. The funny thing is that they still have that bootleg feel. They're in the back of the store in hand-lettered bins. The clerks are never sure of the price—is it $1.69 or $1.96? The confusion continues even when you get the damn thing home. Is it 45 or 33⅓? Has it got a different tune on each side or did you cop, by chance, a real promo disc—with exactly the same cut on both sides! Oh, that kills me! Talk about conspicuous consumption! Waste! Wickedness! Picture this big expanse of black vinyl and the music just a little patch in the middle with long swirling grooves leading into it and out—and the same "5:43" on both sides. Heavy!

Actually, we shouldn't laugh these records off. They represent a real victory for the record-buying public. They are easy to handle, good to hear, and a real bargain because they cost just as much to manufacture, package, and distribute as an album that sells for four times as much. What's more, they are an endangered species. The big labels are starting to cut them out now that they realize the threat these discs pose to the record companies' favorite scam—the dirty trick of taking one hit and packaging it with seven misses to make an eight-dollar album. Too bad Ralph Nader isn't more of a swinger; he would see to it that the record buyer was safe from rip-offs—at any speed.

Though the most obvious advantage of the new stretched-out records was that they kept the groove going in the discotheques, their ultimate effect was something far more important: the extension of the whole time scale within which pop composers conceived their music. Practically all the most interesting and valuable disco compositions of the last few years would have been unthinkable in the old format. Indeed, many of the pieces written before the shift to disco mix have profited enormously by being remixed and released in the length that was always natural to them. This is true of many of the Philly hits, which were broken off so arbitrarily in their original form and which are far more satisfying now for having been extended to three or four times their original length. This is true also of the many records that failed when they were first released and have become hits after they were skillfully remixed. The most dramatic example of how such a quantitative change can become a qualitative change is furnished by the recording that I regard as the single most important composition of the whole disco genre: Donna Summer's *Love to Love You, Baby.*

**EROTIC HYPNOTIC**

YOU remember it, of course. It was a record that spun day and night through the autumn of 1975. You couldn't listen to the radio for half an hour without hearing a spacy, sexy, black woman's voice chanting and gasping and moaning, as if in the rapture of

passionate lovemaking. At first it was startling, almost embarrassing—even in this age of rampant pornography. The reason was that no artistic medium has been more oppressively censored than recording. The excuse was the presumed fact that the primary market for pop records is comprised of teen-agers (an assumption that has now been proven false by statistical analysis but which—even if true—should not have barred adults from listening to whatever they pleased). The record companies therefore have enforced for generations a moral code that would make the comparable codes of Hollywood and network TV seem loose and licentious. Just recollect the ruckus that was kicked up by the Stones singing "Let's spend the night together" or the hullabaloo raised a few years since by the Isley Brothers' attempt to use that dull vulgarism, "bullshit." (The offending word was eventually bleeped out, making it far more titillating.) With this tradition of Victorian prudery to combat, it is a wonder that a major record company undertook to distribute the Donna Summer album and a miracle that so many radio stations gave it room on the air.

From the aesthetic standpoint, the extraordinary thing about the album was not so much the fact that it exploited the extraordinarily exciting effect of hearing a woman making love. The astounding thing was that the creators of the disc had composed an elaborate, erotic ritual. The sex ceremony unfolded slowly and deliberately, step by step, until it had reached its climax. Then—astonishingly—it passed beyond the climax to a postcoital trance that reflected back on the whole experience and transfigured it. It was pop Wagner. Experienced in the proper setting, late at night, stoned on Santa Marta Gold, with the mind relaxed and open, susceptible to imaginative voyagings, the grand effect was what we glibly call "cosmic." More than any recording in recent years, *Love to Love You, Baby* restored to pop music its highest goal: the inducement of ecstasy.

The vision that informed the composition was one of the oldest myths of pop culture, the erotic sacrifice—pop's delightfully debased version of the love=death equation. The myth first surfaced back in the days of the Cotton Club, whose speciality was the production of what were then called "jungle shows." The rich and lubricious white slummers would roll up to Harlem in their Pierce Arrows well past the midnight hour, after cocktails, the theater, and supper, when it was time to set the crown on the evening by giving the girls in their cloches and white foxes one last thrill before bedding them down. The jungle shows, designed to fulfill the *nostalgie de boue* of the white clientele, were marvelously cynical entertainments contrived by geniuses like Duke Ellington to exploit the white man's fantasy of primitive black sexuality.

The particular show Donna Summer's record suggested was that horny old classic, the Sacrifice of the Nubile Virgin. Anyone who visited Acapulco in the good old days can supply the rest: the high flaming altar; the implacable-looking priests in their s/m drag; the fabulously lithe and animallike girl, writhing voluptuously in the grasp of the cruel attendants; the drummer enthroned at the peak of the dais, pounding on his skins; the thrilling moment when the desperately struggling maiden is bent over the sacrificial block and pinioned, and the high priest approaches with his primitive knife....The story tells itself to a slow hypnotic rhythm pounded out

upon those jungle drums. It was this ancient spectacle that loomed behind the disco drama as it unfolded from the shiny vinyl, embossed quite appropriately with a palm-tree logo and the word "Oasis."

What no one realized at the time of the immense vogue of *Love to Love You, Baby* was the very interesting fact that it had been recorded in Munich—of all places!—and that its star was a young black singer who had gone to Germany, as so many American singers have done in recent times, to sing *Porgy and Bess* and *Hair*. *Love to Love You, Baby*—produced by a Swiss-Italian, Giorgio Moroder, in a Bavarian studio—was a pioneering effort of what was shortly to be called "Euro-Disco." The tag designates what has proven to be one of the most fruitful sources of the new music: the sophisticated European record producer employing black American artists to create "concept albums." These are vastly more ambitious than American pop recordings because their designers stand back at a great distance from contemporary America—as the British rock bands stood back at a great distance from the America of Elvis Presley and Little Richard—and perceive the larger and more mythic contours of our fabulous pop culture. The oddest revelation about this first essay of Euro-Disco was the fact that the original recording was designed for the American pop record market,

and was, consequently, not the splendidly prolonged seventeen-minute track with which we are familiar but a measly little four-minute 45! It was not until the clever people at Casablanca's subsidiary, Oasis, obtained the rights to the record that someone had the brilliant idea of remixing it and extending it to the length of an entire album side by purely mechanical means. As the old Marxists used to say: "Quantitative differences become qualitative differences." They sure do, Karl!

## TAKING IT OUT

LIKE any serious enterprise, from love to war, pop music is a game. The players sit around a board and make moves. One move begets a countermove, and as the game progresses, the later moves appear to have no connection with the opening gambits. When Donna Summer scored her great success with her first hit, the pop players all over the world sat up and took notice. In Paris, where the tradition of making sexually suggestive records has always existed, a hitherto unknown French record producer named Cerrone, working with an equally unknown songwriter, Alec Castandinos, analyzed the formula for the Summer hit and decided to take the game one step further. The highlight of the original piece had been the sex cries. Now, what was more exciting than the sound of a woman making love? Why, obviously, the sound of two—or even *three*—women making love. Especially to each other! So that this lesbian focus would not reduce the album to the level of a kinky party record, the catholic-minded Frenchman decided to include in the party a man—himself!

Now the trick was getting the foursome together dramatically. Again, Cerrone evinced his advanced thinking by making the women rather than the man the initiators of the orgy. After all, Cerrone had worked as a hairdresser in Paris. He knew the way modern women talk and think about men—how aggressive and out-front they can be. So, why shouldn't the girls pick up the guy

*Giorgio Moroder*

and reverse the history of the gang bang?

Cerrone's album begins with the loud thump of the bass drum, establishing the heart-pounding pulse of the action. At the same instant, one of the girls kicks off the story by exclaiming, "Wow! Look at him!" Then, as the Fender bass starts humping, the girls—who are in some public place, perhaps a discotheque—begin coming on. As they introduce themselves and ask Cerrone about his sign, one of them, who is obviously black, says, "What do I care about his *sign?* I jes' wanna know where he's *at!*"

At this point, the half-audible, fragmentary, cinema-verité conversation is silenced and the violins commence a conventional-sounding romantic theme sung by a female chorus sighing "Love me!" Just when the mood has been established on the sentimental plane of pop song, the romantic violins are whipped off like the participant's clothes. The listener is offered an astonishing glimpse of the action. "Right *there!*" says the black girl, marking her pleasure spot. "Keep it going!" cries out another girl, approaching climax. The third Ms. moans—"Oh, Cerrone!"

The scene no sooner opens than it closes, leaving the instruments to play with themselves through the balance of the side. Like everything that Cerrone has done and been acclaimed for

subsequently (he received no less than five awards at the fourth annual Disco Forum in New York), the record is little more than a naughty cartoon. The cover was the final touch. It shows four life-sized hands, nicely contrasted in skin color and texture, clasping each other at the wrist to form a box. On the largest and most muscular hand is emblazoned in brilliant tattoo: *Cerrone: Love in C-Minor*.

The notion of the female wolf pack roaming in search of its solitary male prey was too titillating to be abandoned after a single essay. Hard on the heels of *Love in C-Minor* came another French record titled *Chase*, whose theme was summarized in the comic-book album cover. On its face, the jacket shows a drawing of some predatory female spacewomen in helmets, goggles, and zippered suits. Their leader, who has a pair of binoculars slung around her neck and a huge pistol strapped close to her crotch, is pointing across the rocky lunar landscape and shouting, "Chase!" When you turn the album over in the direction in which the patrol leader is pointing, you discover a bizarre-looking space station, with a single little bare-headed man running to the refuge of its fortresslike turrets.

Despite its haunting theme melody, *Chase* didn't get to first base on the American market. The next attempt to mine the vein of *Love in C-Minor* was, however, a smash hit. Titled *Love*

*Cerrone (left), Alec Castandinos*

*and Kisses,* it was the work of Cerrone's erstwhile songwriting partner, Alec Castandinos. A living symbol of the international character of the disco world, Castandinos is an Armenian, born in Cairo and reared in Australia, who lives in Paris and does his recording in a British studio, using singers who speak and sing in a typically American accent. Castandinos figured that there was no point in trying to build up another girl to rival the champ, Donna Summer. He decided to project his heroine as a female chorus singing as a single girl. Instead of the mature woman, hungry for sex, the collective protagonist of this new drama was a screaming teeny who taunts, as if in parody of the Summer song, "Don't wanna love ya! You've got nothin' to give, ya jes wanna take!"

Eventually, the tart little teen does submit. Her statutory rape is narrated in a long, suspenseful, and musically ingenious caricature of the sex act. As the insistent bass drum thumps with phallic rhythm, the violins describe a mounting fever chart. With many ups and downs, starts and stops, the red line climbs steadily higher and higher until the climax is reached and the fiddles finish off their erotic tracery with a final flourish of triumph and escape.

Two years after this game of can-you-top-this was initiated, it was again the first player's turn. Donna Summer now made another winning move. This time, rather than performing against a jungle backdrop, the star executed her enticing vocal caresses in a milieu that was just as obsessive and hypnotic as jungle drums, but which impressed the listener at first as being antagonistic to either sex or sensuousness. On this disc, a couple of Moog synthesizers were made to sound like that funky early-twentieth-century factory machinery that employed lots of spinning wheels and slapping leather drive belts. As the Moog, with its kooky timbres (straight out of an animated cartoon), goes round and round in a crazy industrial ostinato, punctuated by the bump of a simulated bass drum and the slapstick sound of a simulated tambourine, Donna Summer stretches and purrs and repeats the phrase "I feel love!" The interpretation of this number is wide open, but one possibility is that the lady is making love to a cosmic vibrator.

The Euro-Disco producers with their concept albums made a deep impression on the emerging disco industry in America. As the new records on

labels like Malligator, Rivard, Crocus, Ibach, and Carrete became available in the hip New York stores (often arriving by way of Montreal), the disco DJs, whose reputations rested increasingly on their ability to read and lead the trends, gave these novel sides a lot of play. The Europeans had an advantage in that they were geared to produce smaller quantities of records and didn't have to worry as much about violating moral standards. European packaging, for example, was so daring that when an American company licensed a new record, often the jacket would have to be redesigned and toned down. Lesbianism was a theme the Europeans were fond of exploiting. One notorious jacket showed two naked girls, one white, one black, romping lasciviously, the black girl laughing uproariously, while her white playmate clutched her bare breast as if in alarm. If the American companies were going to play in the same league, they would have to counter with some strong stuff of their own.

**DISCO DREAM FACTORY**

**S**OON the American studios were buzzing with new projects, new gimmicks, new sounds. Reflecting, sometimes consciously, sometimes unconsciously, the drift toward Hollywood, disco albums began to fall into distinctive genres, exactly like the old movies. Just as you once had jungle pictures, war pictures, sci-fi pictures, and love pictures, so the dream factories of Discoland began to sort their products into the same categories. The records steam with the rank luxuriance of the Amazon, explode with the violence of war between the worlds, crepitate with the kooky sounds of robots or the eerie wail of cosmic winds, or swoon and climax with the cries and moans of women making love against a backdrop of hypnotic drums.

Let's reach into these bins and run off some representative ciné-disco trips. First, the terror trip, exemplified brilliantly by *Devil's Gun.* The overture is a fantasia on themes of paranoia.

First you hear the sound of gas escaping, as if from an air lock, an Aqualung, or a giant rocket straining for release. Then the beat begins, like a powerful machine switched on—heavy, insistent, relentless. Next, a piano plays some chilling chords while an ominous electronic plectrum begins running mindless mechanical scales. As the countdown proceeds, a Fender bass starts thrumming a telegraphic one-note riff, like a desperately repeated SOS. This urgent signal is picked up and reinforced by a symphony of brass and strings. Spooky female voices are now added to the mix, vocalizing eerily above and behind the driving doomsday machine, which has now worked itself up to blast-off frenzy. Finally, at a point that would be midway through the conventional 45, there is a sudden tympanic explosion, and the "song" begins.

An ogreish bass intones: *"Fee Fiiiie! Foe Fuhmb!* Yo lookin' down da bar-rel o' da de-bil's gun!" Hot on the heels of this house-of-horrors voice come, one by one, like characters in a morality play, all the ghetto voices made famous by Motown: the chorus of strident amen girls, the urgently exhorting preacher, the falsetto male soprano. As each one enters, he or she piles another note of terror or admonition on top of the madly galloping nightmare.

Like so much disco music, this composition builds to shattering climaxes without offering any resolution of its excruciating tensions. The record goes round and round like a perpetual-motion machine. It ends with neither denouement nor transcendence. Nothing can stop it but the conventional fade—which, in fact, does *not* stop it in a discotheque because the ever-alert disc jockey has another record coming up on his second turntable that will continue the mad journey to the end of the night.

Another standard trip today is *space.* Sci-fi auras, cosmic winds, and robot voices chanting oracular messages have become standard properties, and the disco arranger occasionally achieves with them effects that are weirdly beautiful. Consider *Magic Fly,* an arrangement of a Middle Eastern-sounding tune recorded originally by a group called Space. Performed by Kebekelektrik

**139**

on T.K. Disco, *Magic Fly* opens with a passage of naked industrial rhythm, topped by the high-pitched clink of a steel anvil struck with a brass mallet, that could have been lifted from the score of *The Iron Foundry*. After this percussive prelude has established the beat by driving it like a railroad spike into your brain, the disco pulse commences. On top of the bumping, belly-dancing bass drum is imposed a bass Moog that is doing the double bump. Like one of those accordion-extended boxing gloves familiar from Rube Goldberg cartoons, this aggressive mega-beater pummels your body until it's time to blow your mind. Then, one of those eerily swelling epileptic auras—used in sci-fi films to denote the presence of the supernatural—comes wailing down an imaginary wind tunnel to materialize suddenly as the melody. An exotic and imposing Bedouin strain played with great plangency on an electric guitar whose sound has been electronically distorted, this Semitic anthem projects an image of bizarre beauty—Lawrence of Arabia riding across the lunar desert mounted on a stainless-steel camel.

## DISCO DROIDS

**T**HE most drastic and fascinating exploitation of disco's new machine aesthetic is found in the music of Kraftwerk. The publicity shots of these four young men make them appear to be impersonating four superstraight, short-haired, tie-and-suited German engineering students posing for their graduation picture at some technical *Hochschule* circa 1955. Their aura of scientific monasticism is echoed in their music, which is purely electronic and abstracted from the sounds and rhythms of modern technology. They use the Doppler effect of streaking streamlined trains; the *whoosh!* of a passing Mercedes on the *autobahn;* the tweets and beeps of the shortwave radio; and even the mysterious crackling sound of static. Kraftwerk—literally "power plant"—is dedicated to the celebration of the machine and hence of that

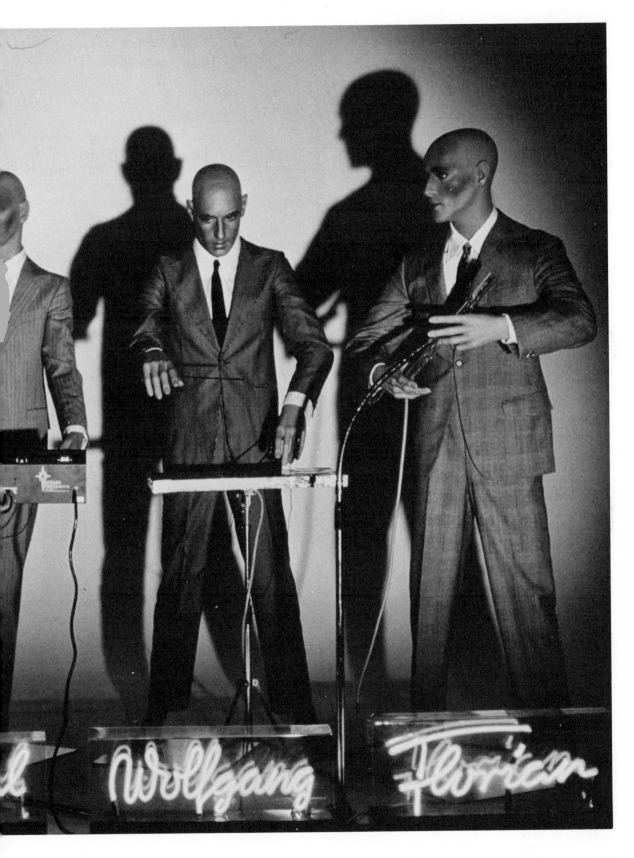

machine-age culture that is the *bête noire* of every Brillo-headed hippie. Instead of being machine wreckers, the Kraftwerkers are machine idolaters —and machine makers.

The band's big disco hit, *Showroom Dummies,* combines the genres of horror and dehumanizing technology to produce a chilling tale of industrial folklore. The theme is that stock legend of German literature, the doll or automaton that comes to life. The mood is established by a melancholy little tune: sad, wistful, schlemiel-like, a *Yiddische lied,* if you please, twanged out a note at a time against a mechanical back beat that evokes the image of the bass-drum beater and castanets inside the core of a carrousel. Starting forth from this weird background, the Voice proclaims: "We are showroom dummies." Then, in a rigidly strophic song, the mechanical man recounts the mechanical tale of the showroom dummies who break their glass to walk through the city and enter a dancing club.

By making such a profound identification with the mechanical, Kraftwerk has become a human machine and in fact this is how the group refers to itself—*Die Mensch Maschine.* The relationships between the human machine, the robot, and the dummy are obvious here, as is the threat that someday the robots will break their electronic shackles and take over the world. What is novel is the suggestion, implicit in all of Kraftwerk's work, that when that dread day arrives, the difference between the robots and the humans may be reduced to nothing. Europe and America are rapidly spawning a race of wax-featured young men who compliantly fill many service roles and spend their evenings dancing in discos to electronically engendered signals. It may be hard someday to tell the men from the droids.

**T**HE background for this new obsession with machines, robots, and sci-fi fantasies was a radical shift in popular consciousness which occurred during the mid-seventies. The time machines that had been programmed during the days of the hippie to carry us back to the turn of the century, "where everything's happenin'," were now abruptly reprogrammed to rocket the imagination into the THE TWENTY-FIRST CENTURY. The Tiffany glass and grandma clothes were put back in the antique shops. People started living in industrial spaces and admiring industrial objects. The new theme was industrial chic.

Nothing exemplified this trend more perfectly than the new disco music, which was a highly

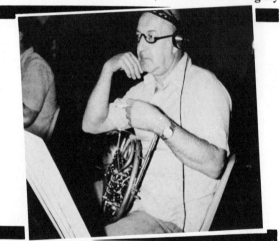

contrived, supersophisticated electronic artifact. Never has there been a music that owes less to the individual or even to a class. Though the music business, locked into traditional patterns of show-biz exploitation, has struggled with all the arts of huff and puff to make disco performers into stars, the medium has remained ineluctably its own message. The truth is that disco has no stars, no creative geniuses, no inspired composers, virtuosos, or even personalities. Rather, it is a collaborative endeavor, a triumph of art and engineering, drawing on the talents, skills, and ideas of hundreds of faceless workers. The disco sound is its own and only star.

The simplest way to understand this new product is to step into the studio and follow the manufacturing process like the stages on an assembly line. The studio world of New York City is centered on the West Side of Manhattan, where the blocks of decaying tenements and grimy factory buildings look like they'll collapse at just the sight of the wrecker's ball. Yet when you make your way through the gaggles of winos and platinum-haired black hookers who hang out on the spattered old stoops and you enter one of these blighted buildings, you feel like you've stepped inside the command station of a space-ship. The control booths with their sweeping consoles and fleet admiral's chairs, their bewildering stacks of amps and equalizers, their gargantuan tape rolls and dramatically raked monitors suggest the planetary authority of Big Brother.

When you look through the huge plate-glass windows into the recording studio, you get another image, that of a geodesic dome or curi-

ously carpentered weather station on the Alaskan tundra, with walls and ceilings canted every which way and mikes suspended like bottles of intravenous fluids. When the players begin arriving for the session, the image shifts again. These shleppy-looking old dudes toting battered-looking instrument cases resemble a klatsch of pinochle players more than they do pop musicians. One guy has brought his sixteen-year-old son to see him work; another old dude with white hair-wings and half-glasses introduces you to his cute little granddaughter. When they settle down to tune up, they start chewing on cigars and drinking from bottles of beer. One cat has even

brought along his dog, like a night watchman or a lonely hack driver.

Appearances are deceiving. Though these guys may look like they room at a welfare hotel, some of them earn $100,000 a year. Though some of them appear to have trouble bending over far enough to tie their shoes, they are the most nimble instrumentalists in the world. Though they laugh and joke a lot, they've all broken their asses working their way up year after year inside one of the most highly competitive, tightly cliquish professions in America. Hardly old hacks who couldn't do anything else, many of these men held down front-desk jobs under Toscanini and Reiner or were sidemen of Benny Goodman and Woody Herman back in the days when symphonic music and jazz were the most challenging worlds any musician could enter. These guys gave up the symphony and the jazz band not because they couldn't hack it but because playing the same stuff year after year got too easy, too boring. Also, they wanted the money. They discovered that you couldn't buy a split-level house in Jersey and send your kids to college and take an annual vacation in Europe on orchestra scale. So they became freelancers.

As they became successful in their little world, their appointment books turned black with dates. They found themselves doing two and three jobs a day, rushing from studio to studio, stashing bass fiddles and drum kits in lockers all over town so that they could accelerate their merry-go-round pace. In a single day, they often went from a Pepsi jingle to a conga-bongo soul session to the twenty-two-stave score of Richard Strauss's *Also Sprach Zarathustra*, known in the trade as *2001*. Working all these jobs for all these contractors with all their different ideas of music and performance, these men received the most exhaustive musical education that can be obtained. Eventually, they became encyclopedias of music and part of New York's most valuable human resource.

Unlike the rock 'n' roll boys, who hire a studio at $150 an hour from midnight to eight in the morning for an entire month just to scratch out one primitive-sounding album, these old dudes work fast and proficiently. They can take one look at a handwritten scrap of music, slip on their headphones, and with a metronomic click track playing in one ear and a symphony with half its notes missing playing through the other, they can, on the first take, knock out the trickiest rhythm or the most demanding technical tour de force. What's more, if the copyist fucks up or the conductor gives the wrong downbeat or the arranger isn't happy with his work, they can correct the mistakes, ignore the wrong cues, and give the producer a half-dozen new ideas that work better than the ones on the chart. If worse comes to worst, they can do what they did in their jazz days—they can *improvise*. No matter what they're paid, these guys haven't time to monkey around. If they're called for "three and a possible hour," that's all they'll play. Then they're packing up and walking out for the next date.

Their only gripe was that for years they got no credit whatsoever. They were said to be overpaid robots who couldn't turn on an electric guitar, much less a theater full of screaming teenies. Pop music was aimed at the youth generation; and if you were going to kill the kids, you had to be a long-haired freak who drank nothing but Tequila Sunrises and had to be fed through a straw. That was the attitude in the music business till disco came along. Then, overnight, the picture changed. Pop suddenly became the most demanding instead of the most simplistic music made, and only these old dudes could cut the mustard. Now the laugh is on the youth generation. Night after night, the kids jam into the discotheques to hear this wild, way-out space music that picks them up and hurls them around like clothes inside an automatic washing machine. And who's turning them on? Who's got them flipping out of their gourds? Who are the hottest musicians in the game? Your Uncle Nebisch, dear, the session man.

**A** perfect illustration of the skills and flair of the New York studio musicians is the story of how one of the most brilliant of all disco albums was produced: Meco's *Star Wars*. Domenick ("Meco") Monardo is a small, keen-witted, and energetic man who worked for years as a studio trombone player. When the disco fad began, he joined forces with one of the top studio arrangers, Harold Wheeler, and a former engineer for Motown, Tony Bongiovi, to form a record-producing company. They had an

initial success with Gloria Gaynor; then Meco got the bright idea of doing a disco version of the score for *Star Wars*.

Monardo, a science-fiction fan, saw the movie at the 10:00 A.M. show the first day it opened in New York. The next day he went back and saw it three more times. The first time, he hadn't even noticed the score. The second time, he realized that the composer, John Williams, had done an excellent job, working with a mixture of Elgar (=Empire) and recollections of World War II soundtracks. The trouble was that the movie was so damn busy that the music got lost. Meco went over to the Colony Record Shop on Broadway to pick up the sound-track album, which had just arrived; he couldn't wait to get home and put it on his turntable. When the music started playing, he experienced a shock of disappointment. It was just a straight symphonic reading, not a realization of the action-comic world of the picture. Why, there weren't even any sound effects: no rocket engines, ray guns, explosions—nothing!

Meco's mind began spinning. He picked up his phone and called Neil Bogart, the boss of Casablanca records. Bogart said that it would be a good project for Casablanca's new subsidiary, Millenium. Millenium agreed. A fast deal was made over the phone. The next step was to translate the score into disco-ese and to start working out the production ideas. Meco wanted to go big: sixteen horns blaring out the martial music, thirty or forty strings soaring with the love theme, synthesizers and sequencers chattering like robots, and, at the end, a fantastic space-age dog fight with sensational sound effects. If they were going to cash in on the idea, however, they would have to throw the album together overnight.

As the arranger, Wheeler, worked around the clock, calls went out to all the best studio players in the city. The drummers got the first call and started laying down the rhythm tracks with nothing but a click in the ear to hold them together. Then it was the turn of the brass, the strings, the woodwinds, each section called in separately and recorded on a different set of tape tracks. The most advanced recording equipment was employed, which allowed the engineers to punch out a mistake and rerecord in the same spot without going back for another take. In this manner, section after section of the complex score was put together in five hectic days. Soon the big melodic passages were complete. The success of the album, however, would depend not just on the broad dramatic strokes but on the ingenious detail of the novelty numbers. The best of these was the section in the smuggler's cantina at Mos Eisley. In the picture, while the main characters plotted their escape, a hot little combo of furry-faced mutants blew some goofy jazz.

Meco decided to exploit this section for all it was worth. To get the effect he wanted, he called a quartet of sax players and had them play the tune at half-tempo; then he accelerated the tape to distort the sound—and out popped the corny but irresistably swinging sound of a rickey-tick Charleston played by the Chipmunks! Next, he called in his best percussionist, David Carey, and played the track for him. As Carey stood in the empty studio listening to the take through headphones, he got his orders from the booth.

"Okay, Dave, the next part is thirty-two bars for vibes. We don't have any music here, so make something up. Ahhh, play like Lionel Hampton!" Carey waited for his cue and with no preparation he started improvising. In the next ten seconds, he laid down one of the best hot-mallet, hard-swingin' solos that had been heard in years. To an old jazz fan, it brought back those glorious days when the great Hamp would enter spectacularly from the back of the Strand, tossing his mallets high in the air and catching them again

until he reached the stage, where he took off on *Flyin' Home.* Everybody in the booth cracked up!

When the album was released, its single went to No. 1 on the charts. Night and day for weeks, every radio in New York played that marvelous bit where the Space City Syncopators do their razzmatazz; then the hottest vibe player in town plays his dazzling concerto for heavy metal. Soon nobody could make a disco album without a clangorous vibe solo. Even Lionel Hampton, when he got his next recording date, gave Dave a call.

By the season of 1976/77, disco had become

**145**

the new entertainment trend in New York. The underground years had revolutionized the medium. Instead of a discotheque being a giant jukebox pouring out the hit tunes of the day, it had become participatory culture's answer to the movie theater and the television studio—an automated entertainment installation that offered specially prepared sound and light shows that were ideally suited for partying and dancing. The discotheque was back to being a private club, yet the qualification for admission to the club was not membership in a social class or celebrity pantheon but rather a genuine love for the scene. Disco costuming was not the bizarrerie of the fashion freaks but the stripped-down outfits that were best suited for working out hard on a dance floor.

The typical disco was no longer an elaborately decorated bar or supper club but an industrial space down in the Garment District. The partying was just as wild as it had been at any time in the past and the orgiastic exploitation of sex and drugs had become commonplace. The difference was that as drugs and sex became elements that were taken for granted, there was more pleasure derived from them and fewer casualties. As for the Mob and its evil rackets, there were now ways to run a discotheque that kept the hoods at arm's

length or cut them out of the scene entirely. All the necessary ingredients for a new explosion of discomania had been discovered and skillfully combined. Now all that was lacking was the catalyst.

## THE EXPLODE-IMPLODE BUSINESS

**A**CTUALLY, there were two catalysts, enough for a two-stage explosion. The first was Studio 54, the second, *Saturday Night Fever*. The first furnished a triumphant demonstration that the new concept of the discotheque would work on a grand scale. The second articulated forcefully the image of the new disco fan as a pent-up kid seeking a stage on which he could assert his pride in being young, good-looking, virile, and sexually glamorous. If Studio 54 proved that all the Beautiful People were eager to exhibit themselves under the colored lights on the dance floor, *Saturday Night Fever* showed

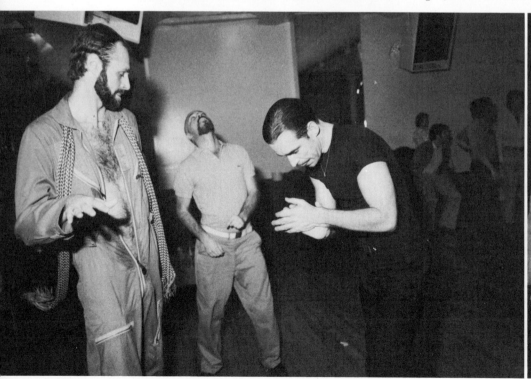

that the Beautiful People weren't the only ones who were beautiful.

Though the movie opened many months after Studio 54 became a byword for New York entertainment, it reflects the disco scene of an earlier period, well before the current vogue. In the winter of 1975/76 a well-known journalist accompanied by a distinguished illustrator happened onto a discotheque out in Brooklyn called 2001 Odyssey. How two such highly sophisticated types found their way to such an obscure dance hall is a story in itself.

The story begins with the author of the piece, Nik Cohn. He was known as the writer of *Rock from the Beginnings* and the cocreator (with the illustrator Guy Peellaert) of *Rock Dreams*. The first book established Cohn as one of the very few commentators on rock that combined an intimate knowledge of its principals with a detached and mocking attitude towards its vastly inflated reputation. *Rock Dreams* exaggerated the caustic tone of his first book and amplified it into a garish vein of pictorial satire. The book purported to show the evolution of rock by drawing its heroes and myths in a pictorial idiom derived from the pub shots, fan magazines, penny postcards, and billboard graphics appropriate to a teen-agers's

imagination. But what the book really did was to trash rock and make it appear from start to finish, from its innocent origins to its lurid and decadent decline, a history of vulgarity, grossness, perversion, and madness. Though the book was fascinating, it was thoroughly disgusting; its "teen dreams" were either idiotic bubble-gum cards or nightmares. Cohn, having vented his spleen and taken his revenge upon the people who had betrayed his own dreams, turned next to the search for the current youth generation's pop fantasies.

He propounded a theory to Clay Felker, the editor of *New York* magazine, to the effect that there existed at this time out in the hinterland of the boros a new generation of kids who neither knew nor cared about the heroes of rock and whose life-style was totally different from that of the sixties. This new generation, the product of hard times, was much closer in spirit to the kids of the fifties. Instead of running away from home and dropping acid and talking revolution and meditation, they plodded along like good little proles, doing what they were told to do all week; then on Saturday night, they exploded. Felker liked the idea and sent Cohn forth to make the flesh word. Milton Glaser, the magazine's art director, suggested that McMullan, the illus-

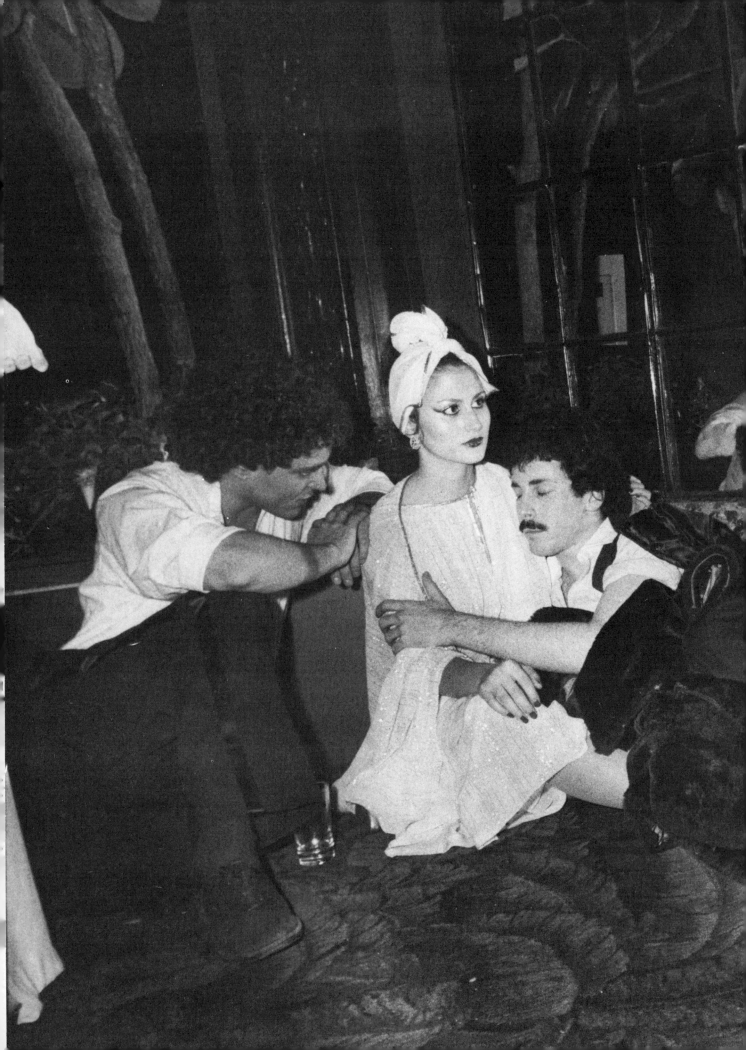

Though Cohn's story provided much of the material for the movie, it was his theory rather than his observations that imbued the film with its animating principle. Cohn had postulated that once a week the new generation "explodes." No explosions were recorded in the article. The hero was supposed to be the best dancer in the neighborhood but his dancing got only a quick phrase or two. He was sought after by girls, but except for one half-hearted attempt at sex, which was quickly and casually abandoned, he didn't make love. Though there were hints of impending violence directed at the local weirdos and Puerto Ricans, there was not so much as a fist fight. The dominant note from the drill-like dancing to the grim rituals of containment was self-conscious repression. Instead of saying that the kids explode, the story said they *implode*. When the screenwriter, Norman Wexler, got hold of the story, he rehashed it so that it produced a whole chain of explosions.

## DISCO GOES HOL·LY·WOOOD!

**W**HAT Wexler did with the story, we all know. He made it pure Hollywood. He discarded Nik Cohn's sinisterly choreographed phalanx of Faces and substituted a gaggle of goofy guys out of *Grease*. He turned the suggestion of the hero's family, which consisted of sisters and a widowed mother, into a TV sit-com with a schlubby, unemployed construction-worker father who degrades the boy and violates his narcissistic glamour. Instead of threats or even suggestions of violence, Wexler pulled out all the stops, sending a car crashing through the windows of a Puerto Rican hangout and a tipsy kid plummeting from the Verrazano Bridge. Nik Cohn's piece was informed by the myths of *The Wild Ones* and *Rebel Without a Cause*, the relevant archetypes; Wexler's script was a pastiche of so many bits and pieces of tired old celluloid that it could have been used for a final recognition test in a film appreciation course.

The worst and most unpardonable thing that Wexler did was to inject into this drama of puerile machismo, this Mafia boot camp, a "love interest." One of the great beauties of Nik Cohn's work had been the way he had depicted his self-absorbed dreamer as totally indifferent to women. In the subliminally homosexual, post-

adolescent world he had painted, girls were anathema. They were, as they are in all purely male societies, symbolic of the "unclean" quality of emotion. Cohn's drama had been played out on the pure level of stoic anomie; his Faces were all deadpan. Having Tony sit in the front seat of the car while the animals gang-bang the girl in the back seat is not the idea at all: It makes the hero seem resigned or indifferent instead of romantically aloof. Worst of all was the dreadful bitch that Wexler injected into the plot to be the ravishing hero's dancing partner and soul mate. No actress could have made sense of this confused character: one minute a scolding high-school marm, the next a hot tango dancer, the next a goony name-dropper and Ms. Malaprop. The least the casting director might have done was to choose a girl who looked appealing, one who was young and attractive and infused with some of the excitement of "liberated" girls. Instead, he picked an actress who looked old enough to be the hero's aunt, starved down on yogurt so that she could pass muster in a leotard in a dance studio mirror. Ech!

As a number of critics pointed out, the screenwriter didn't trust his story enough to let it stand by itself. He had to crosscut it with a half-dozen distracting subplots that led nowhere and proved nothing. As an example of the art of screen writing, *Saturday Night Fever* stinks. Still, the writer did one thing right. He took Cohn's theory about the dull work week and the Saturday night explosion literally. When John Travolta stepped on the lurid electric floor of 2001 Odyssey (laid there by the Hollywood people so the joint would look more like the movies' idea of a discotheque!) he *did* explode!

His dance solos were the climax of the film, if not of the stupid story. What these routines projected were the fantasies of heroism, which in the original story were just vague, half-articulate fantasies. Though Cohn worked wonders with the lights and shadows of his milieu, he never believed in his own characterization of the hero as a great dancer who "had once appeared on *American Bandstand*." Cohn was dance-deaf: He saw disco dance as nothing more than an exercise for Spartan helots. And similarly, he caricatured the black band that played in the disco, who were in fact the Crown Heights Affair, one of the best disco bands of their day. (Why do unmusical people insist so often on writing about music?)

Norman Wexler had a little show-biz in him. He grew up in an earlier generation that had a lot of exposure to show dancing. He cleared a way for the hero onto the floor and then let him do his stuff. Good for him! Without those stagey but thrilling routines and the score by the Bee Gees, the movie would have been a soap opera starring John Travolta. Travolta met the writer half-way by going out and learning how to move. We're always being told by the professors of theater, such as Dean Brustein of Yale, that modern actors have no technique and won't submit themselves to the discipline that Olivier endured when he trained himself to pad around like a nigger for *Othello*. It would be hard to imagine another actor of modern times who could have succeeded so well at the extraordinarily difficult task of impersonating a brilliant dancer. (After the film triumphed, a nasty dispute developed over the question of who taught Travolta how to dance. The show's choreographer, Lester Wilson, made a TV commercial for himself—showing those cardboard steps you lay on the floor!—claiming credit for the achievement. Then, the *SoHo News* printed an interview with a smart-sounding young fellow named Deney Terrio that told the real story. Terrio revealed that he had spent four months with Travolta going to discos and getting him to try hundreds of different steps and moves, selecting those which looked best and which the actor could master. When the original director, John Avildson, was fired and replaced with John Badham, Terrio was dropped from the project and not even given a credit.)

Travolta's performance as Tony was one of the most satisfying things that's been seen on the screen in years. He negotiated the quirky, clumsy script like the nimble dancer he was portraying, coming up a winner in every frame. His great appeal was not so much his sensuality as his marvelous and inviolable innocence, the very quality that Nik Cohn had been seeking in his anthropological search for the new fifties. Travolta was beautiful—there is no better word. His sweetness and sensitivity was something that earlier generations could only imagine in women. Narcissism in our society is a trait associated with women; but in Latin societies, with their male beauty-shop culture and their preening *pappagallo* stance, the male is the bird of beautiful plumage. Travolta didn't even need scenes like the one in which he readies himself for the big night by making an elaborate toilette in his room, a boudoir decorated with pictures of the pale-faced Pacino. He embodied ideally all the sweet, dumb, vulnerable, and erotic charm of the youth of—not Bay Ridge, for Chrissake!—but Bensonhurst, where the Mafia atone for their sins by erecting soaring cathedrals consecrated to the Holy Mother and her son above the two-family houses.

When *Saturday Night Fever* hit the movie houses across the country, disco became a watch-word. Thousands, millions of young people and old saw themselves on the silver screen and bought the clothes, styled the hair, and put on the attitudes that would make them the Tonys of their own little world. Overnight, any little joint with a bar and a patch of dance floor started advertising itself as a discotheque. Pretty soon, everything was coming up disco, from the Ice Follies to the roller rinks, from the cruise ships to the cruising bars, from TV soap operas to TV commercials.

## THAT OLD HUSTLE

THE movie revived the Hustle, even though one of its most disappointing features had been the partnered routines, which were right off a TV choreographer's pipe rack. The Hustle wasn't any big deal, just a revival of the traditional Latin dance rhetoric with a couple of "new" gimmicks, like the Lindy twirl. Still, the dance was suave, graceful, and sexy. In the old Hollywood, it would have provided a vehicle for marvelous stepping and walking-on-clouds fantasy. In the new Hollywood, hung up between *verismo* and entertainment, the dance didn't come off even as well as it does in lots of New York discotheques. The one hip thing about the movie treatment was that it connected the big nights in the local disco with afternoons at the local studio.

The dance studio in New York isn't what it is in Atlanta or Wichita. For years thousands of people in New York who wanted to be dancers or maybe just wanted to come on like dancers had been going to these places and working out under the eyes of some very good professional teachers. New York was a city of dancers and lots of them took themselves pretty seriously. When the

*The Family Travolta*

movie broke, the dance instruction studios in the Theater District, the places like Jo-Jo's Dance Factory, began to do a land-office business in "Latin Percussion." Next to jeans and jogging shorts, the most important item in every woman's wardrobe became her leotard.

The ultimate effect of the movie was something no one would ever have believed possible: the disco-ization of rock. The rockers had always been disco's most contemptuous foes. As Vince Aletti quipped in a piece titled "I Won't Dance!" the rockers regarded disco music "as silly yet

somehow subversive drivel worth only a passing sneer." Robert Stigwood's house band, the Bee Gees, were not typical stick-in-the-mud rockers; they were musical chameleons, remarkably adroit at adapting themselves to whatever was the going thing.

## STAYIN' WITH IT

WHEN the Bee Gees came to fame, their models were the Beatles, whom they mimicked so successfully that teeny-boppers used to go into record stores demanding songs by the fab four that were really written and recorded by their Australian echoes. What comes through in all the best work of the Bee Gees and lifts it above the level of its often trite material is a peculiar vocal tone and spiritual stance that stabs straight to the heart of contemporary sensibility. Their note—which melded so well with Travolta's characterization of Tony—is one of naked sincerity and vulnerability, of injured or abject innocence, pleading with quivering lips against the stern sentence of fate or rising to a peak of chilling assertion in a high white WASP wail. This bleak, piercing, keening Celtic upper register appears time and again in their songs to electrify the listener and to compel him not just to hearken to their message but to engrave it on his heart.

In their latest avatar, as heroes of the boogie-down disco scene, the Bee Gees evinced all their accustomed cleverness and abstractive ability to condense the familiar gimmicks of the black-inspired beat for the feet. *Stayin' Alive,* the traveling music that opens *Saturday Night Fever,* is a classic bit of car-radio, summer candy-store music, neatly bifurcated, like the hero's soul, between the mindless scuffle of the big-city streets and the urgent inner voice of his soul, focusing all his barely adequate spiritual energies just to keep going, just to stay alive. The most exciting moment in the score is the one tune in which the Bee Gees depart completely from their own lachrymose history and from that of rock in general:

the marvelous hit titled *You Should Be Dancing.* Taking off from the same musical clichés that were employed till recently only by black disco groups or by K. C. and the Sunshine Band, the song ascends swiftly into the bizarre Witches' Sabbath atmosphere of the postmidnight coke-and-popper-crazed discotheque. By employing skillfully all the tricks of overdubbing, echo chambers, and studio-orchestra phantasmagoria, the Bee Gees composed an incantatory and bat-flitting paean to the new American Nighttown. After the obligatory Puerto Rican drum break —if we were in a real discotheque, the dancers would at this point break out their teeny-weeny corncobs filled with amyl nitrate and blast each other into the oblivion of the Big Rush—the Bee Gees make a final entrance that is pure uncut ecstasy. Flying in across the bongo-conga-cowbell ruckus of the band comes the high white wail pushed to agonizing intensity—like the scream of a cat being immolated in a microwave oven.

The Bee Gees's sound-track album shot to the top of the charts and stayed there for months as over twenty million copies were sold around the world. This stupendous number far exceeded the greatest hits of past times. Coupled with the earnings from the film, which are now more than one hundred fifty million dollars, it has made an enormous impression on the entertainment industry. Quite apart from the tremendous boost *Saturday Night Fever* gave to the disco business, it confirmed the thinking of many knowledgeable men that the future of the entertainment industry lay in an eventual coalescence of films and the records into a giant entertainment combine. It also suggested that the dominant partner in such a combination would be the record companies because they are more affluent and more closely in touch with current trends. Not only do they have the capital to finance pictures, but they also have under contract the stars required by the new vogue of movie musicals. Even more important, they have the ability to increase enormously the profits of any such venture by linking the release of the movie to the release of the sound-track album so that one hand strengthens the other and both are clasped aloft triumphantly in a joint, multimillion-dollar publicity campaign.

The power of this parlay to make even the most mediocre material successful at the box office was demonstrated shortly after *Saturday Night Fever* by *Thank God It's Friday*—known to disco fans as "Thank God It's Over!" A regression to the worst days of beach-blanket movies, a hideous caricature of the whole disco scene, this bit of technicolor trash made money even in the face of sneering reviews and competition from much better films. So much for disco in Hol-ly-*woood!*

## STUDIO À UFO

THE first time I stepped into Studio 54, I was flooded with a powerful sense of déjà vu. I felt that I was reading a page of *Brave New World.* Far from seeming bizarre or unbelievable, the great industrial theater impressed me as being precisely what discotheques should have always been but never were: a wild party at the River Rouge Plant. Instead of feeling dwarfed under the ninety-foot ceiling, I felt wonderfully elated and composed. The spectacle was exhilarating and beautiful. It was all that stuff Tom Wolfe wrote about the electric signs in Las Vegas brought indoors: the worship of the Mighty Watt.

My delight in this mechanical Christmas tree was shared, I soon learned, by everyone. The latest discotheque was not only the most popular, it was far and away the finest entertainment establishment that had opened in New York since Radio City Music Hall. In fact, with its futuristic glamour and soaring scale, it was vaguely reminiscent of America's finest theater. I couldn't imagine what sort of person could conceive such an audacious design. Eventually, I discovered that Studio 54 was the collective improvisation of a number of men and women. It had been thrown up so quickly and spontaneously that it simply assumed the ideal form of the moment without submitting to the dictates of any single mind. It was exactly like disco music: the anonymous product of a team of skilled professionals.

The founders of Studio 54 were a couple of young men who had known each other since college and who had accumulated considerable

experience running clubs and restaurants before they took on the greatest challenge of their lives. Steve Rubell, the club's front man, commenced his business career as a Wall Street whiz kid; then, he left the Street, and borrowing $16,000 from his family, bought a Steak Loft on Long Island. By running faster than Sammy and promising everyone along the track, "I'll pay you tomorrow," he soon piled up a total of six restaurants that now gross $6 million annually. His partner, Ian Schrager, is like the flip side of a hit record. A retiring type, he prefers to work behind the scenes, where he enjoys a reputation for being tough and smart. Nobody seemed to know anything about Schrager, until a muckraking article in *Esquire* revealed, along with a lot of other schmutz and innuendo, that he is "the son of the late Louis Schrager ... a convicted felon ... a known associate of Meyer Lansky ... and second only to Herman Siegel in Lansky's loan-sharking and numbers racket." Go know!

The first discotheque these young men operated was highly successful. It was located in a clubhouse on a golf course in Queens and called—are you ready for this one?—the Enchanted Garden. The enchantment that delighted the guests was not experienced by the neighbors, who eventually ran the men off the property. They complained that the disco was doing all sorts of harm to the community, from running tire tracks over flowerbeds to destroying the peace and quiet of the suburbs. Rubell and Schrager decided to take their operation to Manhattan, where the noise tolerance is higher and where the disco scene was then starting to boom. Their guide through the labyrinth of New York's night life and up the slippery glass slopes of its "high" society was a remarkable woman named Carmen D'Alessio.

Carmen D'Alessio is your classic Latin bombshell. She says, "age is in the mind," and at forty, she lives a lot faster and more joyously than most kids. The daughter of a Peruvian landholder, she was reared on a country estate that was bordered by an Incan burial ground. She appears to have some ancient Inca not buried but very much alive inside her. Her face, with its broad cheekbones, strong brows and bold eyes, a mane of coarse black hair, and a flashing smile, is distinctly Indian. Her work, which is providing mailing lists to restaurants, clubs, and discotheques, also keeps her in touch with many primitive passions and rituals. Her stock in trade is eight thousand color-coded index cards bearing the names of everybody who counts for anything. Each color designates a different category of potential customer: "wealthy, young, gay, powerful, sedate." With the fashionable world at her fingertips, Carmen boasts that she can turn any establishment into an instant success. "I tell you someseen, darling—ze backbone of any club is ze mailing list. Without zat, you end up with ze white elephant." In the case of Studio 54, Carmen provided not only the guests but the elephant.

Among her acquaintances was a German ex-model named Uva Harden, who had been developing a "disco theater" to be lodged in CBS's abandoned studio 52. He had dubbed the place Studio 54 (to match the street number) and had drawn up plans for the hall's conversion, which was to be bankrolled by the Marlborough Gallery. When Marlborough lost its court battle with the heirs of the painter Mark Rothko, and was hit with a $9.2-million-dollar judgment, the plan was scrapped. D'Alessio urged Rubell and Schrager to latch on to the project anyway. Rubell took one look at the immense space and turned to D'Alessio: "Can you fill it?" he gasped. "I weel!" exploded the bombshell.

Just like Arthur, Studio 54 was thrown together in desperate haste to catch the tail end of a fleeting season. Unlike Arthur, which had been a little room with a minimal installation, the old opera house demanded a colossal effort. The budget was pegged at a staggering $400,000. Rubell and Schrager didn't have any coffee growers to back them (though they soon had them as customers). They were shooting for the in-crowd, which might turn up at D'Alessio's beckoning but would never come back again if it didn't find something extraordinary to stay for. Fortunately, New York was rallying so successfully in 1977 that investing a fortune in a discotheque didn't seem as crazy as it might have even a year earlier. The partners made a deal with a liquor merchant in Brooklyn, Jack Dushey, who in exchange for 50 percent of the take arranged a $333,272 credit. Cash in hand, the desperately determined pair went out and hired some of the best talent that money could buy.

Jules Fisher and Paul Marantz, a team of highly successful architectural and theatrical

lighting designers, were put in charge of the stage area; Ron Dowd, a trendy new decorator, was charged with beautifying the lobby and lounge areas. Unfortunately, Dowd's ideas ran contrary to the lighting designer's thinking; the result was that Studio 54 presents one of the most schizzy faces ever donned by an entertainment house. When you walk into the lobby, you're overwhelmed by a Brucknerian symphony of high camp. Towering mirrored burgundy red walls, banana-leaf carpeting, sixteen-foot fig trees. When you've run this gaudy gauntlet and entered the main hall, the scene shifts, as if at the wave of a sorcerer's wand, and you're looking at a huge hangar filled with hard-edged industrial shapes and the maniacal lights of Times Square. High Camp *vs.* High Tech—what a clash!

The incoherence of the design made no difference because the real effect was the one created by the building itself. For the first time in history, a discotheque was not stuck in a cellar or a loft, an old nightclub or a theater. The place was an opera

Studio 54 had a secret inner sanctum known only to
most privileged patrons. The password was: "Let's pl
Phantom of the Opera." The hideaway was a huge ca
underneath the dance floor. Steve Rubell grew so ena
ored of the place that he furnished it with neon sculptur

house! "It's like the story of *Christ in Concrete*,"
chuckles the club's publicity director, the genial
and girthy Ed Gifford. "The old impresario, Fortune Gallo, had put his body and soul into the
place. All we had to do was exhume that *bel canto*
spirit."

The simplest way to articulate the vast space
was through the lighting equipment. The designers hit upon a brilliant and totally original idea:
the so-called chase poles or movable towers of
bubbling colored lights. The idea came to Paul
Marantz after his first visit. He stepped out into
the dark street and cast his eyes up towards the
skyline. There, running up and down, were
the shifting lights of the MONY (Mutual of New
York) sign. Instantly, he had the conception for
the towers that have become Studio 54's
trademark.

By the time opening night arrived in April
1977, Carmen D'Alessio had done her work well.
She had not only run through her eight thousand
cards, but had culled the lists of Andy Warhol;
Calvin Klein, the dress designer; Francis
Scavullo, the fashion photographer; and all her
gay friends from Fire Island. Five thousand invi-
tations had gone forth and the crowds that came
surging into the mammoth hall on opening night
packed it to capacity and beyond. They were the
first of many such overflowing mobs. Though the
press and the media treated the event as casually
as they always do something that they aren't prepared to regard as important, the word spread like
wildfire. Soon the first question that arose at any
social gathering was: "Have you been to Studio
54?"

Once the club got going, it turned out that it
was not only the greatest discotheque in history
but also an extraordinarily popular setting for
every sort of social function. In the afternoons,
the early evenings, on Mondays when the house
was officially dark, Rubell and Schrager found
they could book in an endless number of political
fundraising affairs, celebrity birthday parties,
promotional galas for films and rock stars, and
fashion shows by the greatest designers. There
was no end to the uses to which the dazzling hall
could be put. Not just a bonanza but a whole gold
rush, Studio 54 made millions of dollars with its
cheap automated shows. It sold stacks of costly
tickets for special events, like its New Year's Eve
party with Grace Jones. For this one evening

*clanging pinball machines. Then he dreamed of ...ning it into a Bumpmobile park. Finally, he realized ...t if all his glamorous celebrities were hanging out in ... cellar, his club would lose its principal draw. From ...t time forth, the basement was barred.*

alone, Carmen D'Alessio estimated that over five thousand tickets were sold at $25 a shot.

## ARTFUL DODGER

CURIOUS to meet the prospector who struck this seam of gold. I arranged, one night I won't soon forget, to interview Steve Rubell. Having suffered the customary anxiety attack and wait at the door, I was passed through the clamorous mob and presented to a little guy who looked like a badly wasted sixteen-year-old. Though he played host every night of the year to the most beautifully costumed people in the world, he wasn't exactly a candidate for the best-dressed list. His outfit consisted of raggedy jeans, a Marlboro Man's shirt, orange sneakers, and a moldering green velour jacket. Wrecked chic? No sooner did I meet him than I lost him. He excused himself and darted over to some new face, whom he embraced ardently. After dancing around this guest like a cocker spaniel welcoming his master home, he came back and resumed the conversation—only to dart off again so that he could embrace another group of guests. All night long he did the bunny hug, while I cooled my heels in growing exasperation. "Steve Rubell belongs in an opera house, alright," I thought, "singing the *Largo al factotum:* "Figaro quà! Figaro là! *Figaro! — Figaro! — Figaro!"*

When he returned, he would perch on the edge of a banquette, where his eyes scanned the action as frantically as a security camera tracking a bank robbery. Finally, he beckoned across the room a nice-looking lad dressed in a punk outfit. He had a skillfully drawn cosmetic razor-slash down his cheek, which he had dripped artfully onto his T-shirt. The lad's partner was a nearly life-sized doll. Stevie beamed at him like a proud parent and told me that this oddball came every night to dance with his doll. He praised him for being the best-behaved and most loyal of customers. I forced a faltering smile. (What the hell do you say to someone like this?—"Who's that doll you're with?") Just then Artful Dodger took off again on a dead run across the floor.

## PARADE OF THE FAMOUS PUNIMS

**N**O disco has ever marshaled night in and night out such an extraordinary pantheon of famous people as Studio 54. The club was a paparazzo's flash-lit dream. The celebs volleyed into the club in spectacular bursts—coveys of famous faces would pop up fresh from some dinner party or East Side affair. The wire services and the city desks and the foreign news bureaus soon got hip to that. You could station a photographer in this one club and every afternoon, like the second mail, your desk would be covered with pictures of every newsworthy person in New York cutting a caper at Studio 54. Some photographers gave up all their other work to concentrate on this incredible parade.

As the pictures and stories poured forth, Studio 54 got to be the newspaper equivalent of a soap opera. "Why do you never see Bianca dancing with Mick?" "Doesn't Elizabeth Taylor look old—and fat!" "Who is this cowboy with the Kennedy girl?" "Doesn't Andy Warhol ever smile?" "Why did Margaret Trudeau leave Pierre?" In the age of *People*, Studio 54 was the ultimate peephole.

Eventually, being a "somebody" and being a regular at Studio 54 got to be one and the same thing. Like an appearance at court, an appearance at the discotheque confirmed one's standing in society. When after its first year of operations, Bob Colacello, the omniscient and omnipresent society reporter of Andy Warhol's *Interview,* decided to list all the important, fashionable, or "cute" people he had met in the course of the preceding month, his list was virtually identical with Studio 54's. As he acknowledged, he had encountered most of these toffs at this disco or Régine's. "The party season," he groaned, "which in years past began after Labor Day and ended on New Year's Eve, has continued without stop, reaching, this maddest of Marches, a Saturday-night-fever pitch—every night. Finally, it all became too much, a blur of people partying their lives away, a list of names in tomorrow's gossip columns." Colacello's was the best and most complete list:

## *I HAVE A LITTLE LIST*

Empress Vreeland
Queen Régine
Pope Andy
Count Capote
Elizabeth III
High Highness, Halston of Mt. Olympic
Dr. Giller
Ken Harrison
Marisol
Victoria Hugo
Joe Eula
Barbara Allen
Studio Rubell
Bryan Ferry
Bianca Jagger

Fred di Laurentiis
Mark Shand
Peter Beard
Carole Bouquet
Andrea Marcovicci
Margaret Trudeau
Tom Sullivan
Catherine Guinness
Hickey Hockey
Judy and Rod Gilbert
Vitas Gerulaitis
Richard Weisman
Lexi Brockway
Princess Diane de Bobo
Patient Pierre

Pepe Baldaraggo
The Kaisermans
Chateau Margaux '78
Camilla and Earl McGrath
Isabelle and Freddie Eberstadt
Nenna
Delfina Rattazzi
Francois de Menil
Clarisse and Larry Rivers
Prince Michael of Greece
Maxime de la Mayonnaise
An Italian Mime
Adriana and Brooks Jackson
Vittorio Moltedo
Laura Taddei

Maria Laura Vinci
Mary Magdalen Elliman
Lisa Robinson
David Doll
Unique van Vooren
Livia Weintraub
Marion Javits
The Senator
Franco Ciaro
Craig Brawn
Kevin Farley
Shelley and Vincent Fremont
Gigi and Ronnie Cutrone
Ellen Burnie
Chris Makeout

**164**

Nan Fanfare
Annette Reed
Zip
Zarem
Bob Wiener Schnitzel
Go Polk
Annalindon Morris
Marinara Schiano
Robin West
Yves Montand
Priscilla Rattazzi
Marquis Anthony Portago
Honorable Anthony Russell
Roberto Shorto
Sam Spiegel

Lacey Neuhaus
John Ballato
Hubert Givenchy
Ingo
Ronee Blakeley
Sylvia Miles
Steve Mazoh
Carl Woodstein
Nora Ephron
Liz Smith
Iris Love
Diane Judge
Ara Gallant
Paul von Ravenstein
Apples

Jack Bellini
Marjorie Reed
Kenny Play Lane
Tony Cloughley
John Richardson
Pearl
Bill Blass
Lady Keith
Timothy Leary
Bob Felden
Clive Davis
Kathy Johnson
Alexander Marchessini
Vincent Fourcarde
Joan Fontaine

D'Antonio
Renata Adler
Joanne Dupont
Paul Jenkins
Denise Bouchet
Mr. Fondaras
Claudia Venezuela
Carmen Delicious
Daniela Morera
Guy Burgos
Isabella Lambton
Phillip Naylor-Leyland
Rachel Ward
Stan Dragoti
Cheryl Tiegs

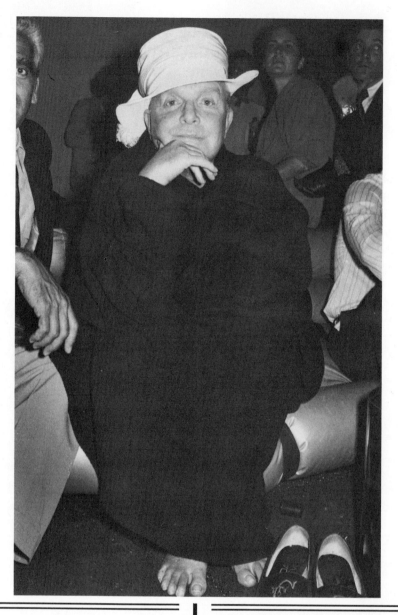

"Wealthy, young, gay, powerful, sedate"? Who's Who? Which is What? Were these the only categories? Were these enough categories? Didn't the categories overlap, exclude, confuse? Oh, it was the ultimate challenge to the pop anthropologist. No wonder Truman Capote went there so often and just gazed.

Another frequent visitor was Diana Vreeland, the high priestess of fashion. As she stood on a vinyl banquette watching the Rockettes wheel out Elizabeth Taylor's birthday cake, she gave an Instamatic interview to the Listing Reporter.

BOB COLACELLO: Diana, it gets more like Pagan Rome every night.

DIANA VREELAND: I should hope so, Bob!

**W**HEN the first great modern anthropologists received the reports of the first great ethnologists—bizarre reports of unimaginable sacrifices and orgies, grotesque ceremonies, and rituals conducted in the depths of remote jungles or in the arid wastes of Australia—they were so fascinated by what they read that they set to work immediately and spent the rest of their lives extracting from these astounding observations the theories that are now taught in every college and university as the ultimate wisdom about humankind. It never troubled these geniuses for one moment that they were dedicating their marvelous minds and imaginations to the study of the most barbarous and primitive people on the face of the earth, because they knew intuitively that all these savage rites and superstitions and mumbo jumbos were the bases of modern civilization.

Since that time, scholars and scientists have raised countless objections to the work of the great pioneers, demanding to know by what right they assumed that such remote and isolated survivals from the Stone Age could be the key to the vastly complex and sophisticated apparatus of contemporary civilization. Those of us who live in the present day, who look down into its depths and see its strange stirrings, know that these pioneers were right. Everything they found in their field reports, from Zambezi to New Guinea, from the Trobriand to the Scilly Islands, has cropped up smack in the midst of the most futuristic cities of the modern world. As Aldous Huxley divined so brilliantly in *Brave New World*, modern man is merely a sophisticated savage.

The epigraph to this book is a classic illustration of this insight. Composed before World War I, at the dawn of modern age, by the great French sociologist Émile Durkheim, it describes the Australian aborigine festival that could be, with few changes, a red-hot disco down in the Garment District. What is remarkable about the passage is not just the link it provides between the rites of savages and the most advanced form of entertainment in the most advanced city of the modern world but the astonishing conclusion that Durkheim draws from the scene; namely, that it exemplifies *the origin of religion*. Read as an isolated statement, this pronouncement seems bizarre and incomprehensible. Restored to the context of the writer's elaborate and scholarly argument, the meaning is both clear and convincing.

What Durkheim contended was that the experience of ecstasy and transcendence, which is the hallmark of all true religious experience, was first engendered by the excitements of such primitive festivals. The ordinary existence of these aborigines consisted of gathering grains and herbs, hunting and fishing—in a word, work. Occasionally, they would gather for a social celebration called a *corroborri*. Herding together at night in the light of torches, they would chant and dance, shout and howl, bang their boomerangs together and twirl their bull-roarers. From the friction of all these sweating bodies and strident voices, from the inciting sounds of the music, from the flashing and flickering of the lights, their emotions were fermented into a highly volatile condition, which Durkheim dubbed, *"l'effervescence sociale."* This yeasty ferment would finally become frenzy. The aborigines would be transformed into manic creatures who did not hesitate to violate even the most dangerous taboos—including incest. They permitted themselves everything because they felt themselves to be in the grip of irresistible supernatural forces. It was at such moments, Durkheim believed, that man discovered the divine.

The history of religion is, according to this view, the centuries-long process of refining and sublimating this primitive inspiration until it eventually assumed the form of the imposing rituals and solemn dogmas of the great world religions. As other students of this theme have observed, even at their most flourishing times the great religions never lost the traces of their primitive origins. What's more, they relaxed their authority periodically to allow the primitive spirit free play, as at Carnival, the frenzied celebration that precedes Lent. Normally, however, the grand façade of organized religion masks the fact that its lofty rites have their roots in the lowest and most savage orgies.

When in the eighteenth century, organized religion began to lose its former authority under the impact of skepticism and the advance of science, the populations of western Europe and America began to erupt again with primitive enthusiasm. The Great Revival produced a wave of frenzied religious happenings that reached a state of mass hysteria. In time, even these strenuous efforts to revive the faith began to lose efficacy, as people instinctively sought other substitutes for their failing religions. It was at this point, in the early nineteenth century, that there commenced the great spiritual shift which has continued at a steadily accelerating pace down to the present day: the religious revolution that supplanted the myths, symbols, and rituals of religion with the myths, symbols, and rituals of popular culture.

Popular culture is a natural substitute for religion in a secular world because it is basically a degraded form of the ancient and primitive religious ideas and practices that antedate Christianity. To the deeply rooted strength of these residues, popular culture has added steadily any- and everything it could borrow from the higher culture. Pop now functions as a surrogate for every sort of culture, especially the arts and humanities, whose greatest inspiration was once religion. Today, both the serious arts and religion have sunk to their lowest ebb in centuries, while everywhere the popular arts are supreme. Mass culture has created mass cult. The rites

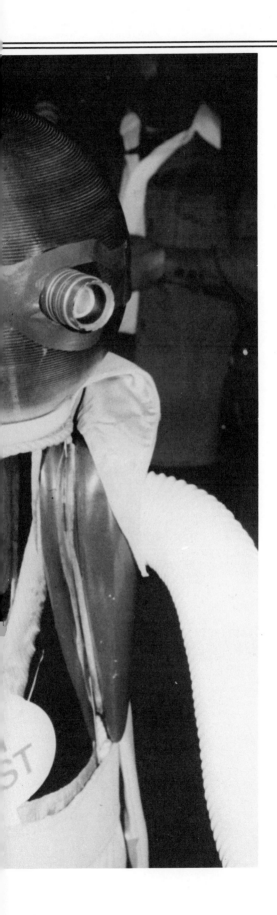

of Sunday have been abandoned for the rituals of Saturday Night.

This state of affairs is profoundly embarrassing to a civilization as highly developed and educated as modern America. We all feel that people should show more enthusiasm for Beethoven's *Fifth* and less for *A Fifth of Beethoven*. Mass cult, we say, is really mass hysteria. In one sense, we are right. Ours is a fallen condition. Yet who can win an argument with history? The fact is that the modern world has cast its old skin and emerged in savage nakedness. No cultural or religious form that does not scrape the bottom and shift with the winds to mirror "the form and pressure of the time" has the slightest hope of seizing and holding the souls of our urban primitives. Only pop culture has displayed this capacity; hence, pop culture is our only functioning culture. As Bertolt Brecht said in *The Three-Penny Opera*: "We'd rather be good instead of gross—but the circumstances do not permit it."

Disco, therefore, is merely the latest manifestation of the new dispensation. Though it has been characterized as the last word in Roman decadence, the truth is that it stands to the present day in precisely the same relationship that rock stood to the sixties, that jazz stood to the twenties, or that the waltz craze stood to the early nineteenth century—when the dance we view as staid was described in the same terms that are being applied to disco today, commencing with "African" and concluding with "zoo."

Conforming, as it does, so strictly to the "form and pressure" of the present day, disco is a reassuringly familiar phenomenon and a perfectly normal expression of our cockeyed world. Especially, it is emblematic of our divided nature: half lab-coated technician, half dancing savage. Of Disco one could say exactly what Voltaire said of God: "If [He] did not exist, it would be necessary to invent Him."

**171**

**Title page:** Sonia Moskowitz

**Facing copyright page:** Sonia Moskowitz

**x–xi:** Sonia Moskowitz

**Facing epigraph page:** Jeff Tennyson

**Following epigraph:** Sonia Moskowitz

**pp. 2–7:** Sonia Moskowitz

**p. 8:** drawing from Martin Hürlimann, *Vienna* (New York: Viking Press, 1970).

**pp. 9–10, 12–13:** Sonia Moskowitz

**pp. 14–17:** 22 Discos by Christopher Makos

**pp. 18–19:** Sonia Moskowitz

**pp. 20–21:** Jeff Tennyson

**p. 22:** Bettmann Archives

**p. 23:** Roger Viollet

**pp. 24–25:** Bettmann Archives

**p. 27:** courtesy of Régine

**pp. 28–29:** Sipa Press/Black Star

**p. 30:** UPI

**p. 31:** courtesy of Vicki Gold Levi

**p. 32:** courtesy of Terry Noel

**p. 33:** illustration courtesy of the Mutual Broadcasting System

**pp. 34–39:** Sonia Moskowitz

**p. 40:** UPI

**p. 41:** courtesy of Olivier Coquelin

**p. 42:** Le Club matches courtesy of Christopher Makos; Hippopotamus card courtesy of Olivier Coquelin

**p. 43:** *Discothekin'* magazine

**p. 45:** top, courtesy of Olivier Coquelin; bottom, courtesy of Terry Noel

**p. 47:** Arthur menu courtesy of Terry Noel

**p. 49:** Wide World Photos

**pp. 50–51:** courtesy of Terry Noel

**p. 52:** UPI

**p. 53:** courtesy of Vicki Gold Levi

**pp. 54–55:** UPI

**pp. 56–63:** Sonia Moskowitz

**p. 97:** Sonia Moskowitz

**p. 98:** illustration and photo courtesy of Olivier Coquelin

**p. 99:** courtesy of Olivier Coquelin

**p. 100:** courtesy of Gifford/Wallace

**p. 101:** courtesy of Denis Wright

**pp. 102–103:** photo by UPI; inset courtesy of Denis Wright

**pp. 104–105, 106, 107:** UPI

**pp. 108–111:** Sonia Moskowitz

**p. 112:** courtesy of Terry Noel

**p. 113:** courtesy of Francis Grasso

**p. 114:** button and matches courtesy of Francis Grasso

**p. 115:** courtesy of Francis Grasso

**p. 116:** button courtesy of Joe Bonfiglio; photo by Ken Kneitel

**p. 117:** Steve Cooper

**p. 118:** Joel Kudler

**pp. 120–121:** courtesy of Philadelphia International Records

**p. 122:** courtesy of 20th Century Records

**p. 123:** courtesy of RCA

**pp. 124–125:** Sonia Moskowitz

**pp. 126–127:** Shoes by Bobby Miller

**pp. 128–129:** Sonia Moskowitz

**p. 130:** courtesy of Disconet, Tom Moulton, and Tom Savarese

**p. 131:** Bobby Grossman

**p. 133:** courtesy of Casablanca Records

**pp. 134–135:** Frank Driggs Collection

**p. 136:** courtesy of Casablanca Records

**p. 137:** Cerrone photo courtesy of Cotillion Records; Castandinos photo courtesy of Casablanca Records

**pp. 138–139:** Sonia Moskowitz

**pp. 140–141:** courtesy of Capitol Records

**pp. 142–143:** Bobby Grossman

**p. 144:** courtesy of Millennium Records

**p. 145:** Steve Cooper

**pp. 146–151, 153, 155:** Sonia Moskowitz

**p. 156:** courtesy of JoJo Smith, artistic director, JoJo's Dance Factory

**p. 159:** Michael Tighe

**pp. 160–161:** Roxanne Lowit; inset photo courtesy of Gifford/Wallace

**p. 162:** Michael Tighe

**pp. 163–168:** Sonia Moskowitz

**pp. 170–171:** Bobby Miller

**p. 172:** Sonia Moskowitz